NO NEUTRAL WORDS

"Sam has written on one of the most important, but often neglected, topics as it relates to pastoral ministry. If we truly believe that our lives are a vapor and one day we will stand before the Lord, then to consider how we use our words as pastors could not be more urgent. In reading this helpful book, you will receive a gracious rebuke and a clear path for biblical change to use your words for life rather than death."

Steven Leatherbury, a pastor of Liberty Baptist Church, Liberty, MO

"In *No Neutral Words: The Pastor's Investment and Stewardship of His Most Precious and Powerful Tool*, Sam carefully, honestly, and winsomely diagnoses and treats one of the most prevalent issues that the church has struggled with since its inception: controlling the tongue and using words for good and not harm. This book will sober every reader, especially pastors, concerning the significance of how they use their words and both the damage and blessing they can cause. If you want to grow in the stewardship of your language for the glory of God, I strongly encourage you to take up and read."

Tyler Sykora, a Pastor of Liberty Baptist Church, Liberty, MO

"You need to read this book, not because Sam tells pastors what they *want* to hear but because he tells them what they *need* to hear, using his words wisely and winsomely throughout. Not only does he challenge us to think more diligently about how we use our words but also to think more diligently about what we take in, what we believe, what we think, who we are, and how we live—all of which inform the way we use our words with those we shepherd. Pastor, you needed a book like this on day one; thankfully, it's not too late to start making every word count."

C. J. Moore, a Pastor of Liberty Baptist Church, Liberty, MO

"Words are powerful. They have the ability to take or give life. What we say can crush or revive those around us. Unfortunately, most pastors haven't given much thought to how to wield their words. *No Neutral Words: The Pastor's Investment and Stewardship of His Most Precious and Powerful Tool* can change that. In his much-needed book, Sam provides pastors with a practical guide for utilizing their most powerful resource. Read this book and implement the wisdom found in it.

Nathan Rose, a Pastor of Liberty Baptist Church, Liberty, MO

"Sam has written a book packed with practical and pastoral wisdom. This is a resource that I will be returning to, referencing, and recommending for years to come. I pray and fully expect that the Lord will use it in the sanctification of many believers as I know he has already done for me."

Bobby Sumner, a Pastor of Liberty Baptist Church, Liberty, MO

"Essential to the ministry is communication, and that reality should sober us. Samuel Bierig helpfully reminds us that Christians—and especially pastors—will give an account to God for every word spoken, written, typed, or tweeted. May the message of this book shape your life and ministry in such a way that more of what you say will give grace to those who hear."

Brandon Freeman, a Pastor of Liberty Baptist Church, Liberty, MO

NO NEUTRAL WORDS

THE PASTOR'S INVESTMENT
AND STEWARDSHIP OF
HIS MOST PRECIOUS AND
POWERFUL TOOL

SAMUEL L. BIERIG

No Neutral Words:
The Pastor's Investment and Stewardship of
His Most Precious and Powerful Tool

© 2021 Samuel L. Bierig
All rights reserved.

ISBN: 978-1-948022-24-8

Rainer Publishing
www.RainerPublishing.com
Spring Hill, TN

Printed in the United States of America

Scripture Copyright: Scripture quotations marked CSB have been taken from the Christian Standard Bible®, Copyright © 2017 by Holman Bible Publishers. Used by permission. Christian Standard Bible® and CSB® are federally registered trademarks of Holman Bible Publishers.

To *Marilyn Geeo*

A most diligent lover and student of Christ, a faithful wife, church member, Sunday School teacher, student of Greek and Hebrew, painstaking editor, and grammarian extraordinaire!

Thank you for all the many hours you invested in me, Mrs. Marilyn. The venture of writing a book only became possible the moment you chose to teach me grammar, syntax, and a thousand other things. You were just the remedy for a few subpar educational years spanning—oh, say—kindergarten to twelfth grade. Any good this book does in the kingdom became possible when you chose to invest your time in the next generation. Thank you.

ACKNOWLEDGEMENTS

I would like to first acknowledge my precious, precious wife Mallory. In the final moments of one of our favorite movies, A *Beautiful Mind*, John Nash, the main character played by Russell Crowe, receives the Nobel Peace Prize, and in his acceptance speech he turns to find the eyes of his wife who stood behind him through it all and says, "you are all my reason." As a Christian, I wish to alter that statement only slightly and tell you, Mallory, you are all my earthly reasons. You are God's love to me come in the form of a covenant wife. And blessed at the gates you should be, for if the tongue be capable and ever flinging daggers, you have caught more of my knives than anyone else. And you have returned only love and unwavering resolve in Christ. You are my evangelical "ride or die chick," babe.

Second, I wish to thank my children for patiently walking with a repentant and sometimes stubbornly unrepentant dad. Abby, Levi, and Owen, you are treasures to your mom and me. I would be remiss if I did not thank my mom and dad for taking me to church consistently. For it is there that I first heard the Scriptures and the gospel.

Whitney Prewitt put more editorial sweat equity in this little volume than anyone else. It is clearer because of you, Whitney! And for that everyone is thankful. You are a gift to God's church.

I chose to ask only pastors and members of Liberty Baptist Church to write endorsements and the foreword. I pray other authors might follow this practice. I have long been baffled that the book industry doesn't make this more a practice given that it is the pastors of one's church who ought to know one's credibility most truly. I thank both Nathan and Brandon for being friends willing to love and rebuke me at some key junctures in my Christian walk. Many thanks to all the pastors at Liberty for speaking truth to me even if it was not always easy.

Drs. Jason Allen and Jason Duesing here at Spurgeon College are gracious enough to provide me time to write and even encourage it. I am forever grateful for these men and their investment in me, their exemplar courage and "followship" of Christ. Dr. Charles Smith has encouraged this project at every turn. Thank you, Dr. Smith.

Last, during my time here at Midwestern and Spurgeon College, I have overseen two different teams. Both of these teams deserve praise for their patience with a quick-tongued boss. Allyson Todd helped me see early on that I had a tendency of hurting interns or staff and remaining oblivious to it. Thank you for your kindness and courage, Allyson.

FOREWORD

BY JARED C. WILSON

These days, talk is cheap, but it lands with amazing expense. If you've ever doubted the biblical word on the tongue being a fire (Jas 3:5–6), you need only check your preferred social media stream to see the ongoing conflagrations being kindled minute by minute. The world is more connected than it's ever been, and thus we have more opportunities than we've ever had to wound others with perhaps our most devastating weapon.

In a world of spin and marketing, self-promotion and self-pity, Facebook comment sections and Twitter mobs, we are drowning in a typhoon of words poorly used, carelessly cast, angrily angled. When words are many, transgression is certainly not lacking (Prov 10:19).

But it's not just "out there" that these fiery attacks take place. Nearly anyone who's spent a decent amount of time in any church can testify to the hurtful application of the tongue, even by brothers and sisters, even by Christian leaders. How subtle is this spiritual fire!

I've been on the receiving end of some very hurtful words. Some were meant to hurt; others did so unintentionally.

Churchfolk can be very simple and unassuming and at the same time absolute ninja warriors with the verbal daggers. Gossip, passive aggression, backhanded compliments. If you haven't been outright attacked by malicious speech in the context of Christian community, you've likely encountered one of those deceptively subtle kinds of attacks.

As a Christian leader, I've discovered that my words have hurt others entirely apart from my intention! Words I meant as lighthearted struck others as demeaning. Words I meant as inspiring struck others as intimidating. Words I meant as warnings struck others as condemnations. Not all offenses should be taken, of course, but a lot more could be avoided if we were all more on guard about our words.

Our words are indeed a stewardship. They can hurt . . . or they can heal. They can tear down, or they can build up. They can bring condemnation, or they can announce forgiveness. They can deliver bad news or good.

This is why I'm grateful for this book. And Samuel Bierig is eminently qualified to write it. More than almost anyone else I know, he is meticulously vigilant about the way he talks. And Sam talks a lot! But having had him as a pastor, as a work colleague, and, most importantly, as a good friend and brother in Christ, I have watched him watch his tongue on many occasions so that he might be a giver of life with his words. Sam treasures the good news of grace, and in this book he will help you also become a deeper and fuller good news person.

Talk is indeed cheap, but the words herein come at the expense of a costly grace. Read carefully.

FOREWORD

Jared C. Wilson
Member of Liberty Baptist Church, Liberty, MO
Assistant Professor of Pastoral Ministry, Spurgeon College
Author in Residence, Midwestern Baptist Theological Seminary

CONTENTS

Preface 17
Introduction: What's in a Word? 19
Part One: The Tongue: A Diagnosis, Prognosis, Prescription, and Remission... 29
   1. Diagnosis: The Pastor's Words and Heart.................. 31
   2. Prognosis: The Pastor's Words and Tongue 43
   3. Prescription: The Pastor's Words and Worship...... 55
   4. Remission: The Pastor's Words and Thoughts.........67
Part Two: Three Guide Rails...79
   5. The Pastor's Conscience, Motives, and Context..... 81
Part Three: Separating Good Talk from Bad Talk 91
   6. The Pastor's Hurtful Words: Speaking Death.......... 93
   7. The Pastor's Healing Words: Speaking Life............. 107
Part Four: The Pastor's Words in the Twenty First Century 123
   8. The Pastor's Social Media Words 125
   9. The Pastor's Funny Words 133
Epilogue...139

PREFACE

I am not the right guy to write this book. When I set out on this project some years ago, I was deluded into thinking I might have my tongue under control and therefore could "speak" authoritatively to the issue. But through the process of writing and the surrounding pressures and circumstances of my life and ministry Jesus in his kindness has brought me low. You need to know this fact at the outset.

It has been said there are only two motivations that prompt writers to take up pen and write. The first is that one is an expert and will help the conversation along if he is heard. The second motivation is altogether different. It is that one wishes to understand and grow in a particular area—to wrestle a problem down to the mat, if you will, knowing he will never understand or master an issue unless he throws himself into the crucible of painstaking, meditative, attentive processing of it. The book and author you have at hand fit squarely in that second category.

I have often wanted to quit this project based on the firm conviction that I am woefully short of the man you deserve to address you on this point. I have, time and again, envisioned those who know me best laughing out loud as their eyes slide across these pages: "Sam, are you really going to lecture me on speaking with thankfulness and kindness after all the sarcastic and hurtful words you've lobbed my direction?" Or something like, "Ha! You? . . . Try taking a dose of your own meds, hypocrite!" Candidly, they are right to question my credibility.

Although I may not be the most qualified to speak in this vein, nonetheless, this issue must be addressed. Therefore, at imperiling risk, I write most urgently to you, pastor, speaking only with the authority and knowhow of one weary pilgrim to another: I fear you may not recognize just how destructive your words may be. I do not sit on high in judgment of you, brother. However, we really do need to have a talk about your words. We are ambassadors, speaking as ministers of the eternal gospel of our holy God, yet we often spew rancor and bitter gall. This cannot be. I am more convinced than ever of the truthfulness of James's words, "Every kind of animal, bird, reptile, and fish is tamed and has been tamed by humankind, but no one can tame the tongue" (3:7–8).

I am no perfectly credible guide, brother, but I am what you've got, and I am persuaded we must address this with urgency. I cannot promise you that I have been or ever will be wholly consistent in my own ministry and life, but I can promise that I will walk alongside you, in fear and trembling, in this sacred and unnoticed journey of stewarding and investing our words for healing instead of hurt.

WHAT'S IN A WORD?

It has always struck me that Paul's first subject of exhortation to Timothy concerns his "speech" (1 Tim 4:12). It seems that Paul's burden in writing was whether or not Timothy's word ministry—counseling, evangelism, preaching, mentoring, etc.— would render a life-giving or death-bringing effect in his congregation.

Another sobering passage for pastors is that great throne room scene from Isaiah 6. You remember the scene: Isaiah is commissioned to preach to Israel but sensed great ruination over his "unclean lips" (6:5). The seraphim cleanse him by placing a burning coal on his lips (6:6–7), saying, "Now that this has touched your lips, your iniquity is removed and your sin is atoned for." Really? Just like that? Yes. Isaiah's mouth represented the whole of his life and ministry, and his ministry was established once his mouth was cleansed.

You and I ought to glean from these passages that our entire ministry rises, falls, and swivels on how we steward and invest our words. The pastor's words, then, are his most effective tool, his constant craft, his glory, and his greatest potential for moral and ministerial demise. Your words, pastor, are a stewardship and investment for which you'll stand and give an account on judgment day (Heb 13:7, 17).

THE STEWARDSHIP AND INVESTMENT OF AN ETERNAL CURRENCY

As a pastor, you probably think and conceptualize of ministry in terms of financial stewardship. Simple enough. You no doubt feel the weight of stewarding and maintaining accountability for your church's financial budget. Maybe you even venture out and extend the pastor's stewardship to include something like a "time budget." I trust you're comfortable thinking in those terms too. You're likely all too aware of how easily time can be flitted away. There is great need to steward, discipline, and allocate your time. Yes, yes, and amen. *But what if I told you there is another budget you might be overlooking altogether?* What if I told you the Lord has given an equally great priority to *this* stewardship as to your financial budget and time budget? I'm referring, of course, to the pastor's stewardship of talk—his "word budget."

THE PASTOR'S ETERNAL "WORD BUDGET"

Most pastors do not think of life and ministry in terms of a word budget, but Jesus thinks you should. In Matthew 12:36–37 he levels his guns at those unregenerate pastor-types of his own day, the Pharisees: " I tell you that on the day of judgment people will have to account *for every careless word they speak. For by your words you will be acquitted*, and *by your words you will be condemned.*" Our words, as it were, function like a cookie-crumb trail betraying an unarguable

WHAT'S IN A WORD?

case against us of our sin and guilt. It's the careless words, the ones we don't imagine to be a big deal, that we must watch out for.

Maybe more than any other passage in all the Scriptures, Jesus's words in Matthew 12 utterly haunt me, and if they don't haunt you too, then you've not yet properly wrestled with his argument. What Jesus has on the line for you and me isn't, "Oh, I goofed," or "I failed to speak charitably." Jesus time warps us into the future to the final judgment where you and I, these Pharisees, and every single person who has ever hazarded a conversation or social media post will give account for every syllable.

The perceptive among us might sense a mounting problem: "Sam, literally no pastor I know thinks in terms of stewarding a word budget!" Bingo. This is why I am writing. What Jesus is saying is that your everyday conversation, counsel, and even social media all roll up to be an enormous investment of words. But keep in mind, Proverbs 18:21 says, "Death and life are in the power of the tongue." All day long you and I make deposits into people's bank accounts, accruing life or death. In everything from interpersonal conversation to social media to our preaching, we invest in the church members we shepherd, our family, and our neighbors either to build up or to tear down—there is no such thing as a neutral word.

Pastor, this moment looms large over your ministry, and you will not be able to jettison giving an account for your word budget. My hope in writing this book is to (1) transform your stewardship of your God-given word budget, and (2) ready you for judgment! And that investment we make in the church members we shepherd, our family, and our neighbors will be for either life or for death. Hence, there is no such thing as a neutral word.

WORDS ARE WHOLE UNIVERSES UNTO THEMSELVES

What is a word, exactly? If they are investments, how do you measure one? What's inside one? Are they measurable like wattage or pounds or money? Why is it that words wield such inordinate power and influence in our lives? These are all important and valid questions. If we hope to wield our words to heal and not hurt, we have to understand what they are and how they work.

Words don't weigh anything physically, yet we'd be foolish to deny that words can weigh the equivalent of thousands of pounds in our hearts and on our ears—haunting us even long after the hearing. Interestingly, words are literally free; they don't cost us a cent. You know the well-worn quip: "Talk is cheap!" However, if that were truly true, why are kind words so difficult for us, and why do sinful words cost us millions in relational capital? Our words may not have physical weight, tangible currency, or measurable wattage, *but we are worse than fools if we go on living as though our words don't possess disproportionate influence on others.*

So, again, what is a word, exactly? Well, words are sticky. Words have a way of velcroing to the crags of our heart and staying with us as permanent fixtures and conversation partners. In this way, words *work* like a song burned onto an MP3 or CD, seared into the material of our memories. We know words exist, but you can't touch them. They aren't physical creatures! They just seem to persist with us, velcroed to us. Oh, sure, you can touch a word printed on a page, but even printed words are just combinations of alphabetic symbols, stand-ins transporting an author's intention. His words serve as windows to look through. The words are a thing themselves, yes, but something—some reality—stands behind the words to communicate concepts, realities, thoughts, and experience. In that sense, words have whole universes of possibilities—meaning, content, and power! Trippy stuff, huh?

When words sensibly line up, they possess the potential to shock, persuade, describe, hurt, command, transport, and raise hope. In the mouth of God, words can spin whole worlds into existence. God speaks and stars burst into existence, burning at incalculable degrees. Mother birds feed their young like clockwork, ants march in perfect alignment, and shorelines go thus far and no farther. And in the mouth of the Son of God, words can even raise men from the dead.

GOD'S WORD AND YOUR WORDS

Consider the first pages of Scripture: when God created all that is, he did it with words. Genesis 1:3 announces, "And God *said*, 'Let there be light,' and there was light." The very first thing God created was light, and he *spoke* it; he *worded* it into existence through communication. When God uses words, they have world-creating, reality-defining, omnipotent physical consequences. When God speaks, it always happens (Isa 55:10–11). His words lack any element of potential: they are only actual. They are the tentacle extensions, outworking, and fruit of his omnipotence, omniscience, and omnipresence.

As part of God's created world, you are, in a sense, words that exist in the mind of God. Within the mind of God in eternity past, you were first thought, then "spoken" in eternity time, and finally actualized in real time. In that mysterium of God, you represent whole rooms of not-yet-actualized potentialities and soon-to-be eventual realities. Again, kind of trippy, but nonetheless true!

Hebrews 1:3 says we exist by the power of the Son of God's word and that he is holding us together at this very moment (cf. Col 1:17). All that we are—when and where we were born, our height, eye color, mental capacity, disposition, and much, much more—was and is spoken into existence by God through the powerful vehicle of *words*. We are the fruition of his mind, every intricate detail that makes you you and me me. Behold the power of God's divine mind, creative and operative with immeasurable and infinite power, creating through the seemingly mere vehicle of words. This truth is both stunning and doxological!

At the same time, as imagers of God, we speak because He spoke us into existence. God deems it glorifying to himself that we image bearers emulate him. As God's words have immense physical consequences, to a far less degree but no less real, the same is true for you and me. While we do not call things into existence *ex nihilo*, we do image God as we create meaning and content through words. So, in the final analysis, it is not so much what is in a word that matters but rather who is wielding it, and in what way, and for what purpose.

WHERE THIS BOOK IS GOING

Considering what we now know of words, the first couple of chapters will likely be uncomfortable for you, brother. But they are foundational for exposing the sinful patterns and various postures empowering that broadsword you call a tongue. As a pastor, you likely have much latent and unexposed pride precisely *because* you are a professional wordsmith—whether verbal, in print, or digitized. You've no doubt learned how to hide from others behind your talk ("I'm too blessed to be stressed in this mess, brother!" or "We just had 374 make decisions for Christ at VBS, which was weird because we only had ninety-three in attendance!"). We're going to get at that pride made evident in your talk.

In the first chapter ("Diagnosis"), I pull no punches and make no apologies. I aim to convince you that you're on the verge of destroying your closest relationships and tanking your ministry through the way you use your words . . . because you are! You may not lose family, ministry, church members, or your closest friends, but we all know that you can limp along in fruitlessness and loveless relationships for years before the death knell finally tolls. I aim to help you see that train wreck before it hits, equip you to dodge it, and serve you, your family, and your church by glancing that blow now instead of getting your skull crushed in later.

In the second and third chapters ("Prognosis" and "Prescription"), I aim to come alongside you and do a bit of difficult heart work. We'll take a long look under the hood of your heart by addressing your motives and deep-rooted sinful impulses. We will discover that the heart of the issue is that you have a worship problem. If you are going to fix your word problem, the Lord will first have to fix your worship problem. I'm praying the Holy Spirit would reveal many unhelpful postures, heart habits, and sin tendencies made manifest in your wordish ways. In time, the Lord will slowly evict your old, hurtful patterns of speech and bring in new, holy tenants who speak truth and healing.

By the fourth chapter ("Remission"), we'll reach the axis of the issue: your mind. What you ruminate on will ultimately become what you talk about. It is a reflex of the simplest kind and unavoidable. We'll look at ways you can repent of your mind matter.

Chapter 5 ("The Pastor's Conscience, Motive, and Context") will provide you with a means to discern sinful words from those that aren't. God has given us a biblically charged conscience, the ability to imperfectly and yet faithfully discern our motives, and has graciously told us through his Scripture how and when to speak varied words according to our context.

In chapters 6 and 7 ("The Pastor's Hurtful Words: Speaking Death" and "The Pastor's Healing Words: Speaking Life"), we will catalogue a list of both death-bringing and life-bearing words according to Scripture. These two catalogues will not be exhaustive, but they will be sufficient for the battle at hand.

Lastly, we'll address the contemporary issues brought about by our twenty-first century context—social media and humor.

Pastor, if you stay the course, I believe the Lord can use this little book, insofar as it remains faithful to Scripture, to bring about more peaceful relationships and more joy in Christ.

CONCLUSION

Hopefully, you have begun to grapple with the concept of a word budget and how words work like investments. Let's conclude this introductory chapter with a thought project: Imagine for a moment that you are given 100 million dollars, and this money is all yours to spend on whatever floats your fancy. The level of responsibility and accountability for that kind of coin, particularly on judgment day, is staggering to me. Nonetheless, what I'm proposing here is that we all have the equivalent entrusted in us; it's just that this currency comes in the form of words.

God has invested in each of us, especially pastors and ministry leaders (Jas 3:1), a massive trust of words, a gift to be wielded for his glory. We, in turn, take that investment and deposit it in others by speaking life or death. Most of us don't stop long enough to truly consider how we expend our allocated verbal currency. How are you investing your verbal wealth, pastor?

I aim to resource and ready you for judgment day. A day where you will give an account for *every single word* (Matt

12:36–37). You've been divinely apportioned a budget of words, and as an undershepherd in the church of the Great Shepherd Jesus Christ, you must learn to *word* wisely. Let's learn how to speak words of life, not death.

PART ONE

THE TONGUE:
A DIAGNOSIS, PROGNOSIS, PRESCRIPTION, AND REMISSION

1

DIAGNOSIS

The Pastor's Words and Heart

Let us frequently remember the shortness and uncertainty of our lives, and how that, after we have taken a few more turns more in this world, and conversed a little longer amongst men, we must all go down into the dark and silent grave, and carry nothing along with us but anguish and regret for all our sinful enjoyments, and then think what horror must needs be seize the guilty soul, to find itself naked and all alone before the severe and impartial Judge of the world, to render an exact account, not only of its more important and considerable transactions, *but of every word that the tongue hath uttered, and the swiftest and most secret thought that ever passed through the mind.*
—Henry Scougal, *The Life of God in the Soul of Man*

Pastor, do you remember the Apostle Paul's protégé, Demas? His story is somewhat disparate and only strings together when we read between the lines and pay close attention to Paul's concluding remarks in a few of his letters. Demas kept company with biblical author supernovas like Mark and Luke (Col 4:14; Phlm 1:24), so we can safely assume he was a fellow laborer in God's vineyard, traveling with and aiding Paul amidst his many persecutions and ministry pressures. If not for the additional intel we find in 2 Timothy 4:10, we would be right to place Demas among the ranks of Epaphras, Titus, and Timothy. However, there in 2 Timothy 4, in some of Paul's final and most haunting inerrant words, we learn that Demas was never actually a follower of Jesus. He was an apostate—a defector.

Throughout Paul's last words to Timothy, we sense the tearing of a titan. He catalogs the personal costs and pain he experienced on account of desertion, loneliness, and hardship—regretting none but feeling all. He requests that Timothy "make every effort to come . . . soon" and bring with him Mark and "the cloak" he "left in Troas, . . . as well as the scrolls, especially the parchments" (2 Tim 4:13). These are the last requests of a gospel giant, seeking the comforts of warmth, fellowship, and the Scriptures. But among these last anguished words, Paul writes of Demas with a detectible wince: "Demas has deserted me, since he loved this present world, and has gone to Thessalonica."

How does Demas go all the way from riding shotgun with Paul to defecting the faith? Answer: one inch at a time. The flesh is weak and eventually runs out of willpower and calories. What exactly was back in Thessalonica that was worth forfeiting the treasures of my Lord, Demas? Was it a woman? Was it money? What was it, Demas?

Demas is a cautionary tale for pastors. He proves that you, pastor, are capable of deluding yourself into complete duplicity. This kind of double-hearted man is a performer. He thinks, does, and acts one way under the cover of night, in the far reaches and environs of his heart. But, outwardly, in the light of polite society, he appears godly. This imposter-actor may successfully fool his wife, children, and even himself; but the Lord is not confused. It's a successful mirage to everyone but the one who matters most. All hearts are laid bare before God, and he delights only in the kind of pastor who fears him and speaks truth in his heart (Ps 15:2).

We've already looked to Matthew 12:36, where Jesus lobs one of the most staggering statements recorded from his earthly ministry. And to no one's surprise, his remarks are leveled at the Pharisees—the imposter-actor-pastor types of his own day:

> I tell you, on the day of judgment people will give account for every careless word they speak, *for by your words you will be justified, and by your words you will be condemned.*

Prior to this, our Lord had just finished landing a haymaker upside the Pharisees' jaw in verse 34, calling them a "brood of vipers":

> Either make the tree good and its fruit good, or make the tree bad and its fruit bad, for the tree is known by its fruit. You brood of vipers! How can you speak good, when you are evil? For out of the abundance of the heart the mouth speaks

Jesus's point is clear. The Pharisees' *words* are like a trail lined with freshly sloughed snake skins, evidencing the true status of the their snakish hearts. For Jesus, the Pharisees' words were incontrovertible evidence proving this conclusion: despite relishing a reputation as godly ministry leaders, the Pharisees were spiritually dead, serpent carcasses. They were like their father the Devil, that ancient dragon, who used his venomous, forked tongue to bring down the entire image-bearing human race (1 John 3:10).

What about your words, pastor? Your words, too, will sit in the witness box and testify for or against you on judgment day. This is Jesus's transcendent implication: these particular Pharisees are a part of the resurrection of the damned. They will receive resurrected bodies uniquely fit to endure a forever life of always dying but never arriving at annihilation, always morally devolving but never reaching the bottom of that grizzly bodily and moral reality. It is instructive for you and me that those who were around these men, and they themselves, understood them to be quite godly! They were that deluded. Jesus gives them an unerring litmus test—their words. This story ought to chill your blood. These religious leaders were caught fast in the fangs of Satan, and we know it by the way they speak.

YOUR WORDS REVEAL YOUR ETERNAL DESTINATION

> Either make the tree good and its fruit good, or make the tree bad and its fruit bad, for the tree is known by its fruit. (Matt 12:33)

One way to further draw out Jesus's meaning in verse 33 is to expand on his metaphor. If you have a brown rot, diseased tree that hasn't produced fruit in years, would it make sense to liberally apply some of that cutesy nutrient spray from the hardware store to its leaves? Of course not! The problem is deeper than a superficial treatment. Something is wrong at the heart of the tree. The root of the tree is dead, and no amount of cultivation or nutrient spray will bring a dead tree back to life.

Paul says much the same in Ephesians 2:1–2: "And you were dead in the trespasses and sins in which you once walked." The evidence of death is one who walks in sin. Our passage in Matthew points, then, to our words and how we invest and expend them as incontrovertible evidence for whether we are alive in Christ or still dead in our sins. The stunning fact that Jesus addresses the pastor-types of his day in this way should jolt you and me. In other words, to be considered godly by others around us does not insulate pastors from the reality that they may be dead and outside of Christ. Those who are "in Christ" will be minted, and continually reminted, formed, and reformed into the image of Christ (Rom 12:1–2). Our words, then, will be the lively leaves of that holy reality. They'll show what we really are.

The sanctification process necessarily means that, on judgment day, Christians will be less sinful than they were the day of their conversion, and uniquely so in their words. How much truer is this for pastors (Jas 3:1)?

YOUR WORDS ARE A REFLEX OF YOUR HEART

What's rolling around in your head will eventually make its way out in conversation, on social media, and in your teaching and preaching: "For the mouth speaks from the overflow of the heart" (Matt 12:34b).

This word "heart," biblically speaking, is a catch-all term. It stands for the whole psychological self. Currently, in most English-speaking cultures, the word "heart" is synonymous with "feelings" (thanks for that, Disney!). But when the Scripture refers to one's heart, it means to encompass not only feelings but the whole internal, non-physical part of a person (i.e., mind, will, beliefs, emotions).

What you *believe* in your heart to be true, valuable, and important drives your *thought life*, which then informs—even dictates—your *feelings*, which reflexively make themselves known through your words. All throughout our lives, we oscillate back and forth between these two poles of belief and feeling. One informs and charges up the other, and round and round we go. Your words, then, are reciprocal—even symbiotic. Just as what you believe, think, and feel affects what you say, your words create who you are, how you feel, and what you believe. *You talk and write your words, but then, somewhere along the way, your words speak and write you; your words create you as you*, as it were. This is the psychology of your spiritual cardiology.

Consider how Proverbs 4:23 speaks about the heart: "*Guard* your heart above all else, for it is the source of life." Or Jeremiah 17:9, which says, "The heart is more deceitful than anything else, and incurable—who can understand it?" The unconverted heart is only and ever hell-bent on speaking death-bearing words, which is the crux of the problem. Our hearts are steering us through life, both in the short and long run. And your words are simply the outward manifestation of what's bubbling up in your heart.

- If your mouth is full of complaining, you have a heart that's full of entitlement and empty of thankfulness.
- If you constantly lash out at people, you have anger in your heart where you should have compassion.
- If your tongue oozes "scarcasm" you have a cynical outlook clouding your wonderment of the gospel.

YOUR WORDS ARE ETERNAL

> I tell you that *on the day of judgment* people will have to account for every careless word they speak. For by your words you will be acquitted, and by your words you will be condemned. (Matt 12:36–37)

Each time I read these verses, I am freshly paralyzed. The diagnosis is grim: my heart is hopelessly wicked and hell-bent on crushing people verbally. You and I *"will give account for every careless word"* we've ever spoken. They're on record in the impeccable and omniscient memory of God. I, for one, have said a lot of sinful, hurtful, disrespectful, blasphemous, and hateful things in my life—both pre- and post-conversion. Remember, pastor, that on judgment day your words will be a traceable cookie crumb trail leading to an undeniable conclusion: You're either dead or alive. Was Jesus King of your life or not? Your words will confirm or deny.

Our words will acquit us when they bear the burden of proof for our life in Christ, or they'll condemn us, displaying our heart's continued allegiance to Satan. The only option is for Jesus to save us.

CONCLUSION

Pastor, have you done a one-eighty on your sin? Are you a Christian? Have you imperfectly yet resolutely turned your back on your sin patterns? Who are you when no one is in your office with you? There is really no point in proceeding until you get this issue solved. There is no special spiritual status in God's kingdom for pastors. You are just as worthy of hell as any lost person in your community, and your ransom was just as costly as that of every church member in your congregation. For us to move forward, you're going to need to be honest about how sinful your talk is. Jesus has been honest with you and moved toward you in the gospel, so you do yourself no favors by minimizing or holding onto your sin. Your death-slinging tongue required the brutal butchery of the Son of God to vindicate you from its effects. Yes, your tongue is that evil. So, get comfortable confessing and looking at the real you in the mirror. Acknowledge you really are that evil and that you really have caused that degree of damage. But know this even more: The Son of God has loved you all the way from heaven, held onto you through the sufferings of Calvary and tomb, and now sits at the right hand of the Father, exonerated and exalted!

To make Jesus Lord means to place the trajectory, direction, and dreams of your life in his hands. He's boss—even of your mouth. Turn from your sin, pastor. If you have indeed repented, then through the person and work of Jesus the Father has taken away every particle and pound of guilt and righteous fury that once hung like a death sentence over your head. The fitting penalty for each sinful joke, ill-advised remark, sinfully sarcastic conversation, social media outburst, and careless word has been laid upon Jesus instead of you. This is cause for worship. Wrap your head and heart around this eternal fact: there is no anger left in God for you. This is life-altering good news. This is the worship fuel you use to fight the sins of your tongue. God, our loving Father, exhausted, expended, and rained down all his righteous fury on his Son instead of on you. It was the only way to purchase you, brother.

TIPS FOR THE PASTOR'S TALK

Pastor, do you look more like Jesus or more like a Pharisee? Matthew 12:36–37 is a tough diagnosis to hear because Jesus is not playing patty cake with these religious leaders. Yet, the pastor who humbles himself before King Jesus has all the hope and promises of God. Colossians 2:13–15 says, "God made [you] alive together with him, having forgiven us all our trespasses, by canceling the record of debt that stood against us with its legal demands. This he set aside, nailing it to the cross." He has wiped your record clean. You will fail, but in your weakness he is enough. Through the death and resurrection of Jesus Christ, God made a way to change your death-slinging tongue into a life-bringing one.

TIP # 1: JESUS SAVES PASTORS FROM THEIR MOUTHS.

You need Jesus to save you from your mouth. You will shipwreck your ministry if you do not take Jesus seriously on this point. Every single word you speak will be brought to light on judgment day, and it will be fixed evidence as to whether Jesus was Lord in your heart or whether the power and spotlights attracted you to pastoral ministry. Hear Jesus's words, fear the Lord, and shudder. It would be a tragedy beyond measure to appear before the judgment seat of Christ having lived your entire life and ministry deluded into thinking you were converted. I plead with you, take a moment and consider your words and what they say about the state of your heart. How do you speak to your wife and children when no one else is around? How do you speak to your staff in emails and interpersonally? Are you saved and struggling toward and in Christ, as any other Christian, or are you playing shadow games? There could be no more pressing question in all the world than what the God of the universe personally thinks of you.

TIP # 2: YOU ARE YOUR CONGREGATION'S EXAMPLE IN SPEECH.

In the introduction we saw that the first exhortation Paul commended to Timothy was in regard to his speech (1 Tim 4:12). Likewise, what example are you setting for the men, women, and children comprising your church? I didn't ask what example do you *hope* to set, but rather what example *are* you setting? If each member of your church were to be your verbal clone, what kind of church would you have on your hands? What would that church exemplify? Would they be more Jesus-like or Satan-like? Would your church be marked by gossip, slander, and backbiting, or would it be characterized by kindness, affirmation, and candor? Our world is so very harsh and loveless, and the Lord has positioned you to unleash healing words on that same bruised and swollen world. Your words are to be a balm, pastor. He has fitted you to be an agent not of destruction but of godly constructivity in the lives of your church members and neighbors.

TIP # 3: YOUR CHURCH EXPERIENCES YOU PRIMARILY THROUGH YOUR WORDS.

When you visit with and disciple church members, how do they experience you? Do they recognize you to be a pillar of wholesome conversation? Are you known for building up the sheep or for criticizing them? Are you simply using your church members to build up "your ministry" by guilt tripping them into bringing neighbors and friends, or do they bring them because through you your members know their neighbors and family will experience Jesus? What a privileged station in the kingdom you inhabit, brother. Make it a hallmark of your ministry to model how Christ speaks. May it be that others feel as though they have been with Jesus after having been with you.

2

PROGNOSIS

The Pastor's Words and Tongue

A few years back I was on a car ride with a few friends whom I love and hold very dear (they will remain nameless so as to protect the guilty!). I don't remember the conversational context, but at some point two of them began slinging some serious verbal mud on one another. It became intense and awkward, especially for me as a reluctant bystander. I attempted to lighten the mood (and maybe aid my friends in sinning less.) by breaking into the quickly escalating disagreement. I said, "Ok, ok, ok . . . cool cool cool . . . now let's all take turns telling one another *one* positive thing about each other. _____, you start us off." The comment was intended to do little more than break up the mounting hostility and bring some levity. But to my shock they stopped and began to say kind, affirming, and complimentary things toward one another. We all did actually! I still don't quite understand how we shifted gears like that, but it happened. In some ways, what proceeded felt artificial and manufactured, but the words of affirmation were anything but contrived. They were alive, powerful, and true—anything but fake.

I learned something valuable through that experience. Most of us, pastors included, are suffocating under our fears, regrets, and inadequacies—not to mention our guilt and sin. Despite the odd origins of that moment, the affirmation was true and lifegiving. All of us were encouraged and lifted despite the goofy and staged feel of it all. Why? Because when we speak words of life to others' through a letter, a text, or a conversation, as long as those words are rooted in love and grounded in reality, we, by God's grace, create life in others. Our spiritual lungs are filled with the pure air of encouragement, affirmation, and thankfulness. We are imaging our Creator. He designed us all with the same gaping hole of discontent that cries out to be filled. It will either be filled with death-bringing words from the world or life-building ones from other Christians. The things we are able—and ought—to affirm about each other are already there; they just aren't often voiced.

After going through the tough work of diagnosing our hearts in chapter 1, now we will call upon our friend and apostle, James, to aid us in a bit of prognostication. James 3:1 indicates that he has in mind church leaders (pastors), anyone aspiring to leadership in the local church, and ultimately the entire congregation. James writes to local church folk just like you and me. His audience more specifically is a cluster of independent local churches strewn throughout the ancient world (1:1). Therefore, we should assume these are saved, local church members battling against the sins of the tongue just like your church members. Although we are separated from them by many a mile and century, James's prognosis is stunningly relevant and on point for you and me.

THE TONGUE: A SMALL OBJECT POSSESSING DISPROPORTIONATE POWER

Again, James first addresses teachers in their role as exemplars in the local church. He says, "Not many of you should become teachers, my brothers, for you know that we who teach will be judged with greater strictness." (3:1) He then turns to address the rank-and-file members in these churches by pointing to a hypothetical perfect man: "For we all stumble in many ways. If anyone does not stumble in what he says, he is mature, able also to control the whole body" (3:2). James argues that we all naturally manifest more ungodliness than holiness through our talk. In other words, even for followers of Christ, it is still sadly the norm that we hurt people with our words. For James, this is a self-evident truth.

If a man can tame his tongue, then, in theory, his whole body would also be disciplined and under control. Ok, James, I don't follow, but challenge accepted. And why is that true exactly? Answer: because the tongue is the most unwieldy of all our body parts—which is saying something! It is the most hyperactive part of us, the part that's least controlled and least controllable. Our words, then, are the means by which we make our true selves known to others and by which we display our true (im)maturity. Our words are the hinge on which our whole lives turn.

To drive home his point, James deploys three different metaphors for these congregations. The first is a horse with a bit and bridle, the second is a ship with rudder, and the third is a devastating forest blaze.

> If we put bits into the mouths of horses so that they obey us, we guide their whole bodies as well. Look at the ships also: though they are so large and are driven by strong winds, they are guided by a very small rudder wherever the will of the pilot directs. So also the tongue is a small member, yet it boasts of great things.

His logic is simple: A small object, like a bridle or rudder, can exercise a disproportionate measure of power and influence over a much larger object of which it is but a part. So it is with the tongue.

THE TONGUE: A WEAPON OF MASS DESTRUCTION

Our words follow us around, and then we follow our words around. It is not much of a stretch to say that our lives *are* our words. With his third metaphor, James takes us to the cliffs of this metaphorical adventure and drops us off onto the jagged rocks below.

> How great a forest is set ablaze by such a small fire! And the tongue is a fire, a world of unrighteousness. The tongue is set among our members, staining the whole body, setting on fire the entire course of life, and set on fire by hell.

Here we must keep in mind James's dual aim to address both the individual church member and the corporate body of the local church. In the daily life of a congregation, a tiny little tongue can set a whole church ablaze with gossip and slander. A small string of words—just a single sentence, sinful, misapplied, and misguided—can set in motion the undoing of a marriage, a friendship, a small group, or a ministry team. James means to summon a bizarre image of a church member scooping out words from deep down in the pits of hell and hurling them wildly at each other, wounding at random. One small flicker of fire can set a whole forest ablaze.

Looking again at verse 6, James also sees the "body" as representative of a person's whole life. The tongue is to the body what speech is to one's life. The way you talk and use your words has the potential to set your life on a course straight for hell ("setting on fire the entire course of life"). In addition to destroying your church and your life, James is clear: your tongue tarnishes everything else, indicating exactly where you're headed.

THE TONGUE: NEARLY UNTAMABLE AND UTTERLY POISONOUS

> For every kind of beast and bird, of reptile and sea creature, can be tamed and has been tamed by mankind, but no human being can tame the tongue. It is a restless evil, full of deadly poison.

James scratches his first-century beard as he ponders, "Mankind has found creative ways to tame nearly every kind of beast in the animal kingdom, but we have yet to tame the tongue." We hold dominion over gigantic creatures. We

NO NEUTRAL WORDS

build skyscrapers and fly spaceships to the moon, but no man has ever tamed that narrow little piece of flesh flapping between his teeth. Why is that? Once again, it's our hearts (Matt 12:34). Our hearts are unruly and blasphemous because we possess an inherited depravity (Rom 5:12) and our hearts are badly diseased (Jeremiah 17:9). We are in dire need of Christ's resurrection power and life.

As we established in chapter 1, our hearts are like rotten fruit trees—stone cold dead and rendered inoperable for producing God-pleasing holiness (Ps 51:5). We are all born in need of a spiritual heart transplant. Jesus describes our unfortunate state: "But what comes out of the mouth proceeds from the heart, and this defiles a person" (Matt 15:18). Our weapon of mass destruction, then, isn't so much the tongue as it is our heart. Our words are but reflexes of our hearts, and the tongue simply follows (Matt 12:34). The tongue mirrors the heart's disposition and posture with meticulous exactness. Until the heart is transformed, we are no more than broken people breaking people—the wounded inflicting wounds on the already wounded.

And this truth is only magnified in importance for pastors. Look no further than Genesis 3 to see that you're more prone to sling death-bringing words than life-giving ones. You don't stand a fighting chance without Jesus Christ gracing you a new heart. James's prognosis for remission without Christ's sanctifying work is, well, non-existent. You cannot be cured by any other means.

> With it we bless our Lord and Father, and with it we curse people who are made in the likeness of God. From the

same mouth come blessing and cursing. My brothers, these things ought not to be so.

James is perplexed by the duplicitous ways of the tongue. How is it that you can glorify God with your tongue, sing with your tongue, preach with your tongue, and then, in the very next moment, turn it into a blowtorch to scorch a fellow image bearer—someone you pastor? How can we turn on our congregation or spouse, cannibalizing them with our words after spending time in prayer only hours earlier? Pastors are capable of spewing rancor at their staff or volunteers before turning their face toward heaven to sing hymns of sweet praise with hands lifted high. James says,

> Does a spring pour forth from the same opening both fresh and salt water? Can a fig tree, my brothers, bear olives, or a grapevine produce figs? Neither can a salt pond yield fresh water.

James doubles down on his prognosis in this verse. He forecasts utter hopelessness without Christ. We see 1) our words are indicative of our eternal state, and 2) if we are indeed in Christ, then we may need to spend some serious time in repentance. We as pastors are going to have to beg and plead with God—through prayer—that he change our hearts so that our words can then change.

At this point you're probably stiffening up with pride. Your sin is pushing back at me, thinking, "This guy doesn't know me! Who does he think he is?" And you're half right. I don't know you. But I know me, and we are more alike than different. We came to Christ from the same place, and he has saved us away to the same safe place "in Christ." Your pride, brother, will cut you off from seeing your sins of the tongue. Since you're a pastor, you are surely quicker on the verbal draw than most, and you're used to controlling the outcomes of conversations to command the room. Because of that powerful reality, you need to take serious stock and a long hard gander at the kind of power dynamics and power plays you employ to "win" conversations and to get your way. This is pride speaking and a massive temptation for you and me.

CONCLUSION

As we move forward through the third and fourth chapters, we will see that, as pastors, it is über important that we discipline and corral our hearts by pushing out unholy mental habits *by* replacing them with honorable, praiseworthy, pure, and trustworthy meditations. Then, and only then, will we start to speak words of life instead of death. It's still going to be a battle of titanic proportions. In the next chapter we're going to address the pastor's need to put off the deeds of the sinful flesh and put on Christ in place of the flesh. What we'll discover is our word problem is not only a heart and therefore a tongue problem, but that our heart problem is a worship problem. Your *word problem* is really a *worship problem*.

TIPS FOR YOUR TALK

TIP #1: STOP LISTENING TO FALSE GOSPELS.

James 3:1 is always a sucker punch for me. The Lord elevates the bar of holiness for pastors to an almost unattainable altitude. Fortunately for you, Jesus is in the business of turning salt ponds into freshwater (3:12). We are properly disheartened if we stare at our deficiencies and constantly gaze at other pastors' projected efficiencies. Pastor, do not listen to false gospels and false narratives. Look to Christ, brother. You do well to forget yourself. Be instead swallowed up in the powerful, glorious, and cosmos-transforming person of Jesus of Nazareth.

His immeasurable perfect holiness, substitutionary death, and death-crushing resurrection is more than you and more than enough for you. Live there, die there, and rise in the presence of your Lord. His person and good news are still unplumbable in their kindnesses and excellencies. You have more affections to cultivate and glean. Don't move on from Jesus to stare at your own record or someone else's. The answer is still—and always will be—that you are transformed by beholding and savoring Jesus.

TIP #2: TALK LESS.

Here is a novel thought: maybe you should focus on talking less. Post less often on social media. Ask questions instead of filling the silent spaces in conversation. Draw people out. They'll likely feel more cared for and invested in. Ecclesiastes 5:2 says, "Be not rash with your mouth, nor let your heart be hasty to utter a word before God, for God is in heaven and you are on earth. Therefore, let your words be few." That is just solid biblical counsel, isn't it?

TIP #3: YOUR WORDS LIVE ON IN YOUR CHURCH MEMBERS LONG AFTER THE HEARING OF THEM.

Your words have great impact on the members of your church. That should cause you to be measured, patient, and calculated. The Lord intends to save you from your sinful tongue and its impact on your congregation. He will heal you. Pray that he will. He hears. He listens. Be on guard against duplicity in yourself first, as well as in those you've permitted into your choir, band, preaching team, small group leadership, and all other ministry roles. Does your congregation see imperfect-but-yet-striving leaders leading them, or do they perceive they are being led by people who are one thing to the face and another behind the back? You may need to confront some of your team on this sin issue.

TIP #4: YOUR WORDS IMPACT THE FEMALE MEMBERS OF YOUR CHURCH.

I sense that communicative, verbal sin patterns, particularly those manifested in verbal and conversational ways, tempt men and women in different directions and ways. I might even venture to say that the content of female conversation trends more in a relational direction than male conversations. While you may not be tempted toward gossip (you probably are), your uncontrolled tongue may lead your sisters in the uncontrolled use of theirs. As a pastor, be on the lookout for gossip and slander. As we've read in James, a tongue spreading slander can do immense harm. Make it a point of conversation with the women in your church. When you hear it, address it quickly with love and firmness (Titus 2:11–3:3). Make sure that you are marked by wholesome and affirming words rather than backbiting and other sin patterns.

3

PRESCRIPTION

The Pastor's Words and Worship

Imagine that you and I are fishing for snow crab on the freezing Bering Sea, somewhere off the coast of Alaska amidst the Aleutian Islands. We're living the dream, making thousands and thousands of dollars, eating crab legs for dinner each night, and embracing the wild beauty of the Bering. It's been an exhilarating season so far.

But then, all the sudden, we hear over the radio that a nasty storm—a small hurricane—is brewing, and it's headed straight for us. We are rightly scared to death. Can you sense it? You think, "Will the Coast Guard reach us in time? Will we die? Who's going to save us? Does anyone care enough to hazard our rescue?"

The storm grows to full swirl all around us. We ready ourselves for the vessel's eventual capsizing. The waves bludgeon the side of the boat. The situation grows more and more and more severe until finally the boat is overturned. We slide around on the slick belly of the ship, clutching onto anything that will keep us out of the icy waters. The more time we spend in the waters, the closer we are to hypothermia.

But then, suddenly, off in the distance you hear the hum of a fast-moving chopper. Your adrenaline surges! WE ARE SAVED! The Coast Guardsmen send down their basket and hoist us into the chopper. We are going to survive! We climb inside the chopper, and, elated, we hug all the Coast Guardsmen. It's as if our lives were snatched from the jaws of death.

Then, in a stroke of sheer insanity, you turn to the hoist operator. You square up. And you punch him right in the jaw. You then leap off the side of the chopper, back into the deathly waters of the Bering Sea, and as soon as you surface, you straightway swim back to the sinking ship and begin climbing back onto its submerging belly.

That's insanity, right?! You'd be clinically insane to pull a stunt like that. You were saved, and now you're heading once more toward certain death. No one would do that, right?

Well, might I suggest that when a Christian returns to his patterns of sin—all manner of wordish sins, to stay on point—that is precisely what he is doing. *You are saved to be saved, Christian pastor*! You don't have to live in the icy death grip of sin any longer!

Let me try another word picture with you: the Christian life is analogous to a glass filled with water. When we become Christians, we are like a glass filled with useless, dirty water. But, after Christ does his transformative work, we become more like a glass of dirty water that has been placed under a faucet that is pouring in clean water. It takes time to clear out old habits, postures, motives, and tendencies, but after a while that old dirty water (e.g., death-producing words) slowly begins to be pushed out and replaced with clean, refreshing, and useful water (life-producing words). This analogy depicts the apostle Paul's typical pattern in his letters. He begins with our beliefs because what we believe dictates our actions.

In this chapter we will see up close Paul's pattern for repentance leading to worship, as exhibited in Colossians, with a focus on the implications of the gospel change that takes place in the Christian life. Paul expends a considerable amount of energy on the words of the individual Christian and how that rolls up congregationally (Col 3:17). So, if we're going to speak life-giving words like Jesus (John 11:43), we are going to have to fill our hearts with his clean, refreshing, and useful word (Col 3:16). Only then will our mouths follow suit and speak words that honor and bring life to those around us.

In this third chapter we want to turn the corner on this sin issue. In Colossians we'll find a prescription for our diseased heart and mouth. First, you need to know that the road to recovery begins with a humble posture as you bow your heart before Christ and plead with him to change your heart. Second, you're going to have to create heart habits of thankfulness, love, kindness, affirmation, and encouragement. These sanctified postures and heart habits (patterns) will then push out and replace the toxic, leftover postures that manifest themselves in your life as anger, slander, filth, covetousness, and greed. Depending on how given over to these patterns you are, you have likely experienced relational and ministry fallout from them already.

You could summarize the big idea of Colossians like this: as the true sovereign of the universe, the Son of God is to be worshiped above all else, unchallenged. Because of this truth, we ought to follow him unwaveringly and make known his lordship in every nook and cranny of our lives. In keeping with his overarching agenda, Paul unfolds Colossians by proclaiming the transformative nature of the gospel in the life of the Christian in chapters 1–2. But when he arrives at chapter 3 he pivots and, much like a doctor, writes out a prescription as to how the Colossians (i.e., Christians, everyday church members) ought to live in light of their redemption in Christ. You could say his point is, "Christians are saved, so be saved!" The gospel is both what we look back on to remember what we've been saved from, and it is the fuel—the example—by which we move forward in the Christian life. We cannot live in such a way that reflects on salvation as though it is not saving! No, we see the death trap of sin as it truly is, and we live in accordance with the gospel. Colossians 3–4, then, serves as the imperative section, the prescription for life in the Spirit, lived out in the Gospel.

LIFE IS DIVIDED INTO WORDS AND DEEDS

In 3:17 Paul boils the whole Christian life down to two things: words and deeds. "And whatever you do, in word or deed, do everything in the name of the Lord Jesus." Remember the introduction chapter? Consider again how little thought most ministry leaders give to the stewardship and influence of their words. We know already that God has invested in each of us a vast stewardship in that we speak millions upon millions of words in a given lifetime. And we know that pastors and ministry leaders bear a particularly high responsibility since we purport to teach in accordance with God's Word. By the Spirit of God giving us this verse, he shows us just how important words are to our lives. Again, your life can be broken down into two areas—words and deeds. That means, pastors and ministry leaders, Christ's honor and name are at stake with every word that tumbles out of your mouth. They count for life or death.

GOOD TALK > BAD TALK: *DO NOT USE* YOUR WORDS THIS WAY

In Colossians 3:8–10 we're told not to use our words for "anger, wrath, malice, slander, and obscene talk. . . . Do not lie to one another, seeing that you have put off the old self with its practices and have put on the new self." This is how you and I naturally use our words outside of the saving and sanctifying work of Christ. And in our quick-tongued society, this is a real problem for pastors and ministry leaders. We are no less susceptible than other members of our church.

I'll bet, pastor, that you sometimes tell crude jokes and laugh when others tell them. We live in a slap-stick, bathroom-humor culture. I am not convinced that these are neutral jokes. This is a tremendous temptation for many, but falling prey to this does not adorn the gospel. Of a different variety, lashing out in anger against your kids, a fellow pastor, or coworker in the ministry does not show mercy as you have been shown mercy in the cross of Christ. Slander is a form of verbal manslaughter according to James (Jas 4:2). It's a type of murder where you attempt to tear down a fellow image bearer in the mind of another, usually with a motivation to lift yourself up in the mind of your hearers. Or consider lying, which is far more prevalent and tempting for me and you than is comfortable to acknowledge. Lying tells a lie about the gospel that saves you from living in mistruths.

What we ought to consider instead is that Christ died so you might live a different life than what's represented in the sins of Colossians 3:8–10. You don't have to live like that anymore. You've put off the old self and have now put on Christ. You are free to extend mercy and not wrath. You are free to speak honorable words and not obscene ones. You can devise plans to honor a fellow image bearer instead of devising and spewing malice. You can encourage and affirm by telling the truth about God's work in a fellow Christian brother or sister, and you don't have to tell lies to appear greater by some worldly measure.

GOOD TALK > BAD TALK: *DO USE* YOUR WORDS THIS WAY

In Colossians 3:12–15 we're told that Christians are to replace words of anger, wrath, malice, slander, obscene talk, and lies with words of compassion, kindness, humility, meekness, patience, forgiveness, love, peace, and thankfulness.

> Put on then, as God's chosen ones, holy and beloved, compassionate hearts, kindness, humility, meekness, and

patience, bearing with one another and, if one has a complaint against another, forgiving each other; as the Lord has forgiven you, so you also must forgive. And above all these, put on love, which binds everything together in perfect harmony. And let the peace of Christ rule in your hearts, to which indeed you were called in one body. And be thankful.

This is the way that a local church is to live out the one-another commands. What Paul expects to be implicitly understood in verses 12-15 is that words are the hinge on which all these Christian characteristics turn. Words are the conduit, if you will, where all these Christianly characteristics and attributes come together. Christians are known to be compassionate, kind, humble, meek, and patient through the vehicle of their words. The realities Paul speaks of here are what typify any given Christian's—including your church members'—speech, and pastors lead the way by their example. We have been loosed from the slavery of a destructive sin nature, and therefore we can speak life instead of death.

FILLING OUR MOUTHS WITH WHOLESOME WORDS

In Colossians 3:16 we read, "Let the word of Christ dwell in you richly, teaching and admonishing one another in all wisdom, singing psalms and hymns and spiritual songs, with thankfulness in your hearts to God."

Our hearts and words are to overflow with thankfulness and singing. We are to admonish one another with wisdom, thus building each other up. That's what our words are meant to do! Our mouths are to be filled with singing to the Lord, and our lyrics are an overflow of thankfulness. Thankfulness for what? God, in his infinite kindness and mercy, showed up in your discipleship and ministry, not as a fearmonger but as one who is slow to anger and abounding in loyal love and faithfulness. It didn't have to be so, but God almighty utilized his limitless power for kindness instead of fury. Thankfulness indeed abounds.

CONCLUSION

So far we've examined the weight of the stewardship of our words and how our words function much like investments in people's lives. There is no such thing as a neutral word (Prov 18:21); rather, all of our words will propound either life or death in the lives of our hearers. This is uniquely immense and weighty for pastors because we carry a higher responsibility (Jas 3:1). We've also seen that the problem is our heart, that each and every careless word we speak will be brought up on judgment day (Matt 12:36), and, according to James 3, our words have great power. Now, having established the difficult foundational work of understanding a proper diagnosis and prognosis, we start down a road to recovery (prescription). In chapter 4 we will look again to the Apostle Paul, this time in the book of Philippians. He'll show us how to guard the gates of our heart and minds that we might form humble and righteous postures and therefore grow in the discipline of stewarding our words for life and not death.

PRESCRIPTION

TIPS FOR YOUR TALK

TIP #1: YOU ARE THE LEAD WORSHIPER AT YOUR CHURCH, PASTOR.

Ask the Lord to put a song of worship and thanksgiving in your heart so you can avoid the sins of slandering your neighbor and blaspheming your God. We are to fill our mouths with praise, and you are charged with the sacred task of bringing order to your local church's singing (Col 3:16). This is a distinct and marvelous trust, brother. Make sure that the words you lead your church to sing are consistent with the words you say out of the pulpit. And sing loudly!

TIP #2: STOP AND CONSIDER BEFORE JOKING.

Pastor, you have the weighty task of speaking life and eschewing words of death. Sarcasm, thoughtless jokes, and mindless comments all roll up to an example for your congregation to follow. Paul tells us as pastors that we are, whether we like it or not, setting the tone and temperature in regard to the communication between our church members. In what particular areas do you need to grow? Compassionate speech? Forgiving speech? Gentle speech? Humble talk? Kind words? Loving emails and social media interactions?

TIP #3: CONSIDER THE STATE OF WOMEN'S MINISTRY AND THE TONE OF THEIR CONVERSATIONS.

Because you will likely spend most of your time among other men, remember to pay attention to the speech of the women of your church. Consider setting up a conversation with the natural female leaders from your church, women's minister (if your church is blessed to have one), and the other pastors of your church in order to discuss how the women of your church are faring in this area. Given James's warning in 3:1-12, it is safe for you to assume that wordish sin patterns are prevalent in your church and, therefore, among the ladies in your church. Challenge them with what it looks like to put on Christ as shown here in Colossians 3. Your ladies ought to be marked by forgiveness, compassion, gentleness, humility, kindness, and love. Is that how you would characterize the ladies of your church? Praise God he is all of these attributes and more. He

PRESCRIPTION

is at work on these women, just as he is at work in you. Pray now for wisdom, patience, and boldness to afflict the comfortable and comfort the afflicted.

4

REMISSION

The Pastor's Words and Thoughts

The sentences that come rolling off our tongues are little more than the final stage of the thoughts and meditations that have been bumbling about in our hearts and minds. What we meditate on and what consumes our thoughts are eventually going to come out verbally or in print.

In the 1979 animated film *Jack Frost*, the dictator-villain Kubla Kraus tries his best to pull off despotism, but in the end he simply lacks the evil gravitas necessary. He is cast as a comical caricature, as funny as he is deluded. At one point in the film Kubla takes center stage to solo forth his song that cleverly divulges his own delusional self-talk:

> I'm Kubla Kraus
> I'm king of all the Cossacks
> But there are no Cossacks to be king of
> There's the rub
> There's the rub
> There's the rub

NO NEUTRAL WORDS

Quite self-indicting, huh? These lyrics allow you to see yourself in the mirror that is "Kubla Kraus." You, too, play false narratives in your heart and mind.

That said, the above is Kubla's first line of self-justification. He immediately, and very comically, confirms for his listener that he can go to great lengths to exonerate himself from any feelings of guilt or fault as king. His next flight into fancy goes like this:

> I'm Kubla Kraus
> I could have been a pharaoh
> But there are no pyramids around here
> There's the rub
> . . .
> I rule with an iron hand
> I get whatever I demand
> I own the people and the land
> So why is it I'm not happy? I don't understand

And with that last question Kubla shows the chink in his mental armor. He displays that he isn't happy, but before he can accept any true ownership for his plight, he rushes off again to the euphoric state of narcissism:

> I'm Kubla Kraus
> I could've been a Rajah
> But there are no elephants around here
> There's the rub
> I'm Kubla Kraus
> I could've been a shogun

> But there are no samurai around here
> There's the rub

You and Kubla are not as dissimilar as you might first think. The ability to justify and construct false narratives is eerily native to you and me. If we skillfully insulate ourselves, we are capable of living our entire lives without coming to terms with our sin. The key to sustaining this sinful insulation game is pushing away any thoughts that would cause you to be humbled and confess that you are sinful. It is the battlefield of the mind where we win or lose the stewardship game for investing words of life or death.

In Philippians 4:8 Paul says, "Finally, brothers, whatever is true, whatever is honorable, whatever is just, whatever is pure, whatever is lovely, whatever is commendable, if there is any excellence, if there is anything worthy of praise, *think* about these things."

The operative word is "think." Paul knows that the real engine room of all that you and I say is our mind. You are going to have to turn your thoughts into fighters if you're going to speak life and not death. You won't drift into self-control. You've got to fight for every single thought (1 Cor 10:5). Brother, you must bring your thoughts under subjection. Capture them for Christ. Your thoughts are the lead indicator as to whether he is Captain and King. Your mind space is extraordinarily valuable real estate—real estate that you have got to fight for because it is the most important real estate you have.

TURN YOUR THOUGHTS INTO FIGHTERS

The mind is a great invisible battlefield. If you don't line up the word of God against your sinful impulses, you will utterly fail in the Christian life—which means you'll continue to go on hurting people with your words. You must get a considerable measure of Bible in your system if you're going to have a fighting chance on the battlefield of your mind. Memorize Scripture. Listen to Scripture. Read Scripture. Hear Scripture preached. Pray Scripture—this is the way.

When tempted in the desert, Jesus met Satan at every impasse with basic Bible verses. That's how he fought temptation. You too must employ your thoughts as legionnaires against your sin. Put them to work in the trenches, and feed your ranks with Bible. To fail to do this, pastor, is to live an anemic Christian life. If you are going to succeed in speaking life into others' lives, you need to take your thought life as seriously as Paul does in Philippians 4:8.

Alongside your intake of Scripture, you're going to have to fight *with* your thoughts AND *for* your thoughts. It's at this motive and pattern level that we either win or lose the battle for healing and hurting talk. As there are no neutral words. It follows, then, that there are no neutral thoughts either.

In Philippians 4 Paul intentionally repeats the word "whatever" for a drum-beating effect. He deploys the imperative mood with "think" or "dwell" on these things, and then he fires off eight different characteristics that all exemplify a Christ-like mind. These characteristics are the rightful inhabitants of that valuable mental real estate referenced earlier: truth, honor, justice, purity, loveliness, commendableness, excellence, and that which is worthy of praise are all habits of thought that ought to permeate the pastor's mind.

Paul knows that deeds—and words end up as deeds in the end—all naturally spring from our thought life. You could say, "as goes the brain, so goes the body." He wants to get your mind right, because if he can get your mind in the habit of focusing on the attributes of Christ, then your words will naturally follow. This is where the principle of Matthew 12:34 ("out of the abundance of the heart the mouth speaks") comes to the fore. If you are convinced in your mind that you may not be saved or that this life is all there is, your words will reflect that reality. However, when the reality sinks in that your true address is in heaven with the Son of God, you will think, live, and talk as though you are with God already here on earth (Col 3:1).

Because of Christ's defeat of sin at the cross, you don't have to live under the death blade of Satan and sin any longer. You have the Spirit of almighty God dwelling in you, and through the Scriptures he is transforming you into the image of his Son and remaking your mind in the process.

THINKING DRIVES TALKING

If you are constantly thinking of yourself in vain, narcissistic, and prideful ways, it is neither "honorable" or "praiseworthy." That is not what Jesus meant when he said, "if you want to gain your life, you have to lose it." In your mind, then, you must replace your narcissism with thoughts and plans to serve others. Your words will follow and show up with kindness, care, and love.

If you struggle with lust, your mouth will likely be filled with inappropriate jesting. This should chasten you to guard your mind by guarding the gates of your mind and your eyes. Exchange unwholesome TV shows, music, and images for wholesome, God-honoring entertainment. The unwholesome jesting will dry up on its own, and you'll begin to speak with courtesy and kindness. You want the soundtrack to your life to be biblically themed, and when that happens you'll find that your focus is centered on "pure" and "lovely" things (4:8).

Let's talk about "excellence" for a moment. If your habit is to cut corners administratively, or to cover up mistakes, or if you don't show up on time, or you work with a noticeably bad attitude, then begin to meditate on the good gift of work. Ask the Lord to give you contentment in your work. And when God changes your heart, you'll be able to rejoice as Paul tells us to here in this passage.

The quickest way to eliminate slander is to focus on that which is "commendable" in others. If you think only on the bad in others, what do you imagine will happen? You'll slander them. Practice affirmation in your mind and heart, and then practice it out loud in public. Your mind matters drive your talk patterns.

CONCLUSION

Conformity to Christ is soul-bending work. Conformity to Christ in your speech patterns, then, requires a commitment to daily warfare on the invisible battlefield of the mind. As we come to the end of this first section, what I wish to convey is that—whether you are diagnosing your own salvation via your words (chapter 1), laying down a hope-filled biblical prognosis for your future with Christ's help (chapter 2), providing a prescription for turning the corner (chapter 3), or seeing your wordish plight in remission by conquering the battlefield of your mind (chapter 4)—this is ultimately about carrying out your ministry work in Christ's ministry work. By modeling good speech patterns, reading God's word, trusting the Holy Spirit to change you, and being a doer of the Word by changing your words to the kind that heal and don't hurt, Christ will inflict great blows upon the kingdom of darkness through you.

TIPS FOR YOUR TALK

TIP #1: THERE'S NO SUCH THING AS A NEUTRAL WORD *OR* A NEUTRAL THOUGHT.

Proverbs 18:21 says, "Death and life are in the power of the tongue, and those who love it will eat its fruits." Every word you speak into the ears and hearts of others is an investment for either life or death. It's not hyperbole to say you've yet to speak a neutral word in this life. Always remember that. Every word is an investment.

TIP #2: PRESSURE SQUEEZES OUT THE REAL YOU.

Pressures have a way of testing you and drawing out of you what was always sitting just below the surface. Out of the overflow of the heart the mouth speaks, so you will be squeezed and tempted to sin verbally anytime the pressure is ratcheted down on you in the church, or with your spouse, parents, or problematic church members. Be watchful and on guard. You know it's coming, so anticipate the temptation that comes with extra pressure. Pray beforehand and ask the Lord to cause you to stop yourself, reconsider, and align your mind with what you know is true before you speak.

TIP #3: BE SLOW TO SPEAK.

That's just good biblical smarts, isn't it? When you're surfing the waves of social media, be thoughtful. Are you edifying anyone with this post? Do you need to verbalize what's skiing around in your head right now? Do you stand to lose more by saying it than you stand to lose by refraining? Take time to consider the fact that every word you're about to speak is going on record in heaven (Matt 12:33–37). Calculate, love, and seriously consider what you are saying. Be slow to speak.

TIP #4: FILL YOUR MOUTH WITH SOMETHING ELSE.

Paul's logic in Colossians 3 is that Christians should empty their lives of godlessness and fill them with Christlikeness. In essence, his argument is that you should fill your mouth with something else. Thankfulness instead of greed, slander, and covetousness. Prayer instead of venom, malice, and crude joking. Singing, affirmation of others, and encouragement instead of slander and negativity.

TIP #5: WATCH YOUR MENTAL DIET.

Probably the most important principle to remember in this fight is that you must watch your mental diet. Draw out good treasure from your converted heart. You probably need to clean out some things you have downloaded to your iTunes or Spotify library or your YouTube account. That's just good, old-fashioned Christian repentance and discipline. It's not legalism. If it is in no way honorable, true, praiseworthy, lovely, commendable or excellent, then delete it. This isn't hard: "let us also lay aside every weight, and sin which clings so closely, and let us run with endurance the race that is set before us, looking to Jesus, the founder and perfecter of our faith" (Heb 12:1–2). What you digest and meditate on in your mind is going to come out in your talk. Guard your heart, for it is the engine room of your whole being.

TIP #6: SPEAK TRUTH TO YOURSELF.

You overcome sin by addressing it with the truth of the Scriptures, so speak truth to your mental impulses. Think through what you are being tempted to say, and then diagnose it by asking, "Is this lovely?" "Is this pure?" "Is this honoring to God?" "Is what I am about to say commendable?" You are a combatant, pastor. Combat your sin. Take every thought captive, and when you've come to the end of your war with sin you will rise in the presence of the master of your fate, the captain of your soul, Jesus Christ.

PART TWO

THREE GUIDE RAILS

5

THE PASTOR'S CONSCIENCE, MOTIVES, AND CONTEXT

There is no silver bullet when it comes to discerning or overturning a pattern of destructive talk in your life. However, the three most useful questions I've found for discerning whether or not I am in process of delivering words that will bring healing or hurt are as follows:

1. Is my conscience bothered by what I am about to say or just said?
2) What is my ultimate motive behind what I am about to say or just said?
3) What is the context in which I am about to say or just said this or that thing?

These three questions do not form a fail-safe inquiry into the matter, but combined they produce a litmus test for discerning whether your speech is pleasing or displeasing to the Lord. If you consistently ask yourself these questions, you will better grasp what you need to repent of and how you can better steward and invest your words in the future for life and not for death. The formula, "what I am about to say or just said," is not accidental. As you know, conversations and our lines of communication to others are progressive and ever evolving. You are delusional if you think you'll remedy your verbal mangle in a short time. You will be hacking away at the roots of your verbal sins until you one day speak with a resurrected tongue. So here is how to proceed until that day.

INFORM AND ABIDE YOUR CONSCIENCE

Your conscience is either charged up with the Word of God or it is not. It would be an utter travesty for you as a pastor to have a biblically ill-informed conscience. Moreover, your conscience is only as accurate and useful to you as it is informed by the will of God through the Scriptures. There is no alternative for the Scriptures pulsing through you. There is no alternative for the Scriptures being the loudest voice in your head. They shape us for good as they mold and inform how we feel and respond to circumstance. Reading and listening to God's words, then, is the key to changing our words. It is also true that everything else we consume (i.e., television shows, music, friends, conversations) shapes our conscience as well. Therefore, we ought to be watchful about what we allow to shape our conscience, because it is ever in process of being informed, conformed, or deformed. When our conscience is informed by Scripture intake, we seek to pay it heed, as disregarding it or failing to live by it in faith is sin (Rom 14:22–23).

THE PASTOR'S CONSCIENCE, MOTIVES, AND CONTEXT

John MacArthur, in *The Vanishing Conscience*, says, "the conscience functions like a skylight, not a light bulb. It lets light into the soul; it does not produce its own. Its effectiveness is determined by the amount of pure light we expose it to, and by how clean we keep it."[1] So you see how paramount it is to have massive dosages of Bible intake.

Your conscience, informed by the Scriptures and in the hands of the Holy Spirit, becomes a mighty means, just as preaching or the Lord's Supper per instance, for bringing you to repentance. Do not seek to silence your conscience when you have spoken unkindly, slandered, or gossiped about someone. Confess and ask for forgiveness from God and the person affected. Jesus already established on the cross that you will sin in such ways, pastor. Kill your pride and confess your sin. You are quite sinful, but Jesus is a great Savior. If your conscience is being informed by the Holy Scriptures, then it is already helping you discern what is pleasing to the Lord. According to Scripture, should you ask the Lord to forgive you for something you said some time ago? Ought you go to, text, or call someone, even now, to ask for forgiveness?

Your conscience is not infallible (Acts 10:9-16), but it is informed. If, while in conversation, your conscience begins to poke and prod you, then stop talking. Pause and consider where the conversation is headed. Don't be afraid to shift gears. Seek to again inform your conscience with the truths of Scripture and do not conform to the fear of man. Should you not be speaking on this particular matter? Should you be filling your mouth with praise and thankfulness instead of whatever verbal sin you've fallen into at this time?

I regularly seek to monitor my conscience while in conversation, and it is not unusual for me to stop mid-sentence and say something like, "Well, never mind... that is not really helpful." My conversation partner may counter and ask that I proceed, which we should expect based on Proverbs 18:8, which says, "A gossip's words are like choice food that goes down to one's innermost being." In other words, you and I, the church members we pastor, and everybody else on earth delights in hearing gossipy intel about someone else. But if your conscience is informing you that you ought to abandon this line of conversation, then do so. Shift gears and seek to bring glory to God through thankfulness, praise, or some other godly manner of speech.

CONTEMPLATE YOUR MOTIVES

Your motives, pastor, are slippery beasts. They often manifest themselves in unsanctified and unedifying ways. You should regularly ask yourself, "What is my goal in saying this?" and "What was I trying to accomplish by saying what I just said?" Were your words for the building up of the person, for the sake of the body of Christ and Jesus's glory, or were they meant to inflict injury? And this is where our motives get slippery. Often we would say our motive was not to damage. But, in hindsight, I often sense that when I have said something slanderous or hurtful, I simply chose to suspend my motives in my mind. In other words, I was tempted to slander, and I wanted to do so, so I did. I chose to avoid checking my motives. I fall to the sin of impatience or anger

THE PASTOR'S CONSCIENCE, MOTIVES, AND CONTEXT

with someone, which in turn leads me to the sin of slander or gossip. Are you motivated to speak by your sinful impatience or anger? Then you can be sure that verbal sin is to follow.

James 1:19 says we ought to be "slow to speak." Might James encourage this slowness so we could be informed by our conscience and discern our motives *before* proceeding with sin? I think so. Are you being motivated by the "fear of man" as you speak (Prov 29:25), or are you operating under the fear of the Lord (Prov. 1:7)? One will produce righteousness, knowledge, and wisdom; the other will produce pain, hurt, and death. Nothing will be lost by slowing down to discern your ultimate motive. The Lord prizes the patient, calculated, and slow of tongue:

o Proverbs 10:19: "When there are many words, sin is unavoidable, but the one who controls his lips is prudent."
o Proverbs 13:3: "The one who guards his mouth protects his life; the one who opens his lips invites ruin."
o Proverbs 17:27: "The one who has knowledge restrains his words, and one who keeps a cool head is a person of understanding."

Pastor, slow down, consider, and then reconsider your motives before you speak. Nothing will be lost in conversation by lingering for a moment. You stand to lose much by barreling into a sinful conversation, but you stand to gain everything, even the smile of God, by patiently discerning your motives. After you've lingered a moment over your motives, then proceed on a holy route, pleasing unto the Lord.

CONSIDER YOUR CONTEXT

In the battle that wages for sinful and holy speech, there are few realities more important than discerning the context in which one is speaking. For example, a father and mother may have occasion to discuss the state of the sin patterns and soul of one of their children. That is a good and proper thing. God has ordained that covenant context to exist, and those parents ought to speak lovingly and frankly to one another so as to raise that child in the fear and admonition of the Lord. Even if it is a hard conversation, it is not slander or gossip if it is motivated by godly ends. Those parents were chosen of God to have that conversation. However, a father and mother who are not that child's parents who discuss the same child's sin patterns and soul may very well be sinning. Context and relationship matter.

Another helpful indicator of context when determining if you are speaking righteously or unrighteously is whether or not the person spoken of is present. This is not a failproof indicator, because it can be very good and proper to speak of a person if they are not present if one has the biblical clearance and responsibility to do so.

With that groundwork laid, if you are speaking among fellow pastors, then there are certain subjects, persons, and situations that you ought to discuss with forthrightness for the good of the flock. You may vigorously discuss a church member's marriage or potentiality for discipline with fellow elders in order to determine how to move forward, but that does not mean you are wise or free to discuss the situation openly or widely among other church members. Context matters greatly. The pastors of a given church have been called of God to shepherd the flock, and together you will discuss all manner of difficult things. Be careful how you vent those things both inside and outside of that particular God-ordained context. Pastors who are married: be careful that you not unduly or sinfully burden your wife with pastoral matters. You are called to pastor the flock; your wife is not. Be careful to protect the sheep in the eyes of your bride. It all comes down to who has the authority—the clearance—to speak in a particular scenario.

CONCLUSION

Discerning your conscience, motives, and context is vital for speaking life-giving words. The three questions presented at the beginning of this chapter, if properly deployed, will help you shift gears mid-conversation and save you a thousand confessions and pains. The better you become at informing and responding to your conscience, being aware of your motives, and knowing your responsibility to your given context, the more helpful and healing your words will become.

TIPS FOR YOUR TALK

TIP #1: PRAY THE LORD WOULD INFORM YOUR CONSCIENCE.

To walk by the Spirit (Gal 5:16), you'll need to walk in the light of an informed conscience. Therefore, you'll need to read and meditate on Scripture. I suggest focusing on the Pauline lists of the flesh vs. the Spirit (Gal 5:16–26 and Col 3:1–16). To impute to you a biblically charged conscience is a miracle and, therefore, a God-sized task. Pray and plead that the Lord grant you a biblically informed conscience.

TIP #2: PAUSE BEFORE YOU SPEAK.

Before you speak, consider what your end goal is. What is your hope? Beyond these good intentions, what is the likely result of these words? Will it be help, hope, and healing—life? Or will it be hurt and hate—death? Before you speak, consider the potential outcomes. Consider your motives.

THE PASTOR'S CONSCIENCE, MOTIVES, AND CONTEXT

TIP #3: CONSIDER TO WHOM YOU ARE SPEAKING.

What is the context in which you are about to release your words? Do you have the clearance from the Lord to speak of these matters or persons, particularly to the people you are speaking to? What do you imagine those you are speaking to will do with the information you offload? Is there good warrant for sharing?

TIP #4: DON'T JUDGE THE MOTIVES OF OTHERS, BUT NEVER FAIL TO JUDGE YOUR OWN.

We are not omniscient. Therefore, we fall woefully short of possessing the ability or right to properly judge the motives of another. The fact that we cannot see the thoughts of another ought to give us pause. It often doesn't, and we may sinfully assign motive to another. At the same time, we ought to question our own hearts at every turn. Our motives are slippery and ever shifting. Hold your motives up to the light of the unerring, pure, and perfect Word of God, and in the luminous light discern the truth about your motives. You will never be perfect, that is certain, but walk in the fear of the Lord and seek to speak encouraging and affirming words as often as possible.

TIP #4: HUMBLE YOURSELF AND APOLOGIZE WHEN YOU'VE SPOKEN SINFULLY.

I myself have a fast mouth and a slow heart. If you're anything like me, and I bet you are, you will need to retract conversations and retrace your steps constantly to discern sinful tendencies. Ask for forgiveness from your wife, fellow pastors, and church members. Humble yourself before the mighty hand of God, confess, repent, and ask forgiveness. Your church members will not think less of you, brother; they will sit in awe of your great God who is conforming you into the image of his Son. In turn, they will witness in you a godly example of humility, and Lord willing, will turn from their own pride, too.

TIP #5: READ *CONSCIENCE: WHAT IT IS, HOW TO TRAIN IT, AND LOVING THOSE WHO DIFFER* BY ANDREW DAVID NASELLI AND J. D. CROWLEY.

To think more on the subject of conscience, consider picking up Naselli and Crowley's helpful volume. It is a short, simple, and useful contribution. Beyond just matters of speech, it will do you a world of good to read it.

PART THREE

SEPARATING GOOD TALK FROM BAD TALK

6

THE PASTOR'S HURTFUL WORDS

Speaking Death

Put off the old self.
—the apostle Paul

My aim in the next two chapters is to highlight, but not exhaust, the primary biblical terms that typify speaking death and speaking life. I hope to clarify and define biblical terms and concepts so that in the heat of the battle you'll be sufficiently equipped to discern your own communication patterns and assess whether they are life giving or death bringing according to God's Word. As a caveat, not all life-giving words are received as particularly sweet or nice. Some words need to be severe and intense.

In Galatians 5:19–21 we see the works of the "flesh are obvious: sexual immorality, moral impurity, promiscuity, idolatry, sorcery, *hatreds*, *strife*, *jealousy*, *outbursts of anger*, selfish ambitions, *dissensions*, *factions*, *envy*, drunkenness, *carousing*, and anything similar." I have italicized any sinful works that assume or necessitate speech to achieve. That is not to say that sexual immorality or selfish ambition, for instance, do not require some measure of speech to undertake; it is more so that I wish to highlight the works of the flesh that seem to be immediately apparent in relation to our words. Words are the very axis upon which these particular evil works turn. In Ephesians 4–5 and Colossians 3, the distinction between sinful words and works is even more deliberate and stark.

In Ephesians Paul flags lying, foul language, bitterness, anger, wrath, shouting, slander, and malice. All these are particularly darkening to the soul and need to be "removed" from the mouth of the Christian (4:25–31), especially the Christian pastor (1 Tim 4:12).

As we considered in chapter 3, Colossians 3:17 divides the action of life into two categories: words and works ("And whatever you do, in word or deed, do everything in the name of the Lord Jesus, giving *thanks* to God the Father through him"). In keeping with that paradigm, Paul dials in on "anger, wrath, malice, slander, and filthy language," encouraging readers to put them away from "your mouth" (3:8). Paul continues, "Do not *lie* to one another, since you have put off the old self with its practices and have put on the new self" (3:9–10).

The one who persists in these unrepentant patterns of sin as rendered in Galatians, Ephesians, and Colossians should not reckon himself to be a believer, as "those who practice such things will not inherit the kingdom of God" (Gal 5:21). No, Christ has saved you not to persist in sin but to wrench it from you, that you might truly live. Now, let us put a few of these terms under the microscope so as to assess the enemy within—the old man who is passing away as we suffocate him with sanctification (2 Cor 5:17).

SLANDER

Slander is what Sanballat and Tobiah do to the people of God in Nehemiah 1–6. They taunt the people of God, see the worst in them, and seek to destroy their reputation and thereby stifle the promises of God. These are not good guys—not the team you want to be on! To "slander" means to speak about one's reputation in such a way as to bring reputational or social damage.[2] We ought to replace slander with affirmation. There are innumerable things to affirm in a fellow image bearer, no matter how far gone into sin! Conversely, there is never a good or sinless time to slander. Put it away.

GOSSIP

In 2 Corinthians, Paul's very personal letter to the Corinthian church, he says, "I fear that perhaps when I come I will not find you to be what I want, and you may not find me to be what you want. Perhaps there will be *quarreling*, jealousy, *angry outbursts*, selfish ambitions, *slander*, *gossip*, *arrogance*, and disorder. I fear that when I come my God will again humiliate me in your presence, and I will grieve for many who sinned before and have not repented of the moral impurity, sexual immorality, and sensuality they practiced" (12:20–21). Paul places gossip among a litany of other verbal sins but also among the ranks of sexual immorality. Gossip can destroy a church, dare I say, quicker than sexual immorality.

To gossip means to share information about a person with people that do not need to know that information, usually without the permission or knowledge of the one who is being gossiped about, with a knowing or unknowing intent to harm.[3] Gossip cannot live in an atmosphere of kindness. Speak with kindness about those who are not present, pastor, and never with an intent to harm. You have a lot of social influence and capital; use it to turn conversations, gently correct, or outright rebuke others away from gossip. It is never proper or kind to gossip about an image bearer or, God-forbid, a church member. Put off gossip.

MALICE

In Psalm 41:5 David says his "enemies speak maliciously about [him]: 'When will he die and be forgotten?'" To speak maliciously is to speak, act, and even strategize in such a way as to bring about harm. Supremely, it is to think up reputational or physical harm, speak that harm, then bring it about socially or bodily. Instead, Christians and pastors ought to strategize, speak, and act in loving ways. Seek to outdo malice with loving acts and words.

BITTERNESS

Bitterness starts in the heart and then proceeds outwardly through our speech (Prov 14:10). Bitterness cannot survive at the altitude of thankfulness. Paul, of all people, had much he could have been bitter about. Imagine if Paul chose to view God's difficult providences in his life the way we often treat ours. He would have been profoundly bitter, but instead we find him in Philippians 4:4–6 saying, "Rejoice in the Lord always. I will say it again: Rejoice! Let your graciousness be known to everyone. The Lord is near. Don't worry about anything, but in everything, through prayer and petition with thanksgiving, present your requests to God." Crowd out bitter words by filling your head and heart with words of rejoicing and thankfulness.

ANGER

James tells us that, "human anger does not accomplish the righteousness of God" (Jas 1:20). So why does God get to be angry, but we don't? The Lord is immutable, *a se*, omniscient, omnipresent, and omnipotent—a perfect and *simple* being so we never need worry that his anger is in error. You and I, on the other hand, have seriously incomplete knowledge and power. Therefore, we are warned to steer clear of fits of anger. We often do great damage in our angry outbursts. Likely, the most painful, critical, and cutting words you've ever experienced came in the heat of someone's rage. Instead, we are—by God's grace—to be self-controlled, cool-headed, and measured in our words, awaiting the righteous reckoning of our Father and not trusting our own (Rom 12:19). To be clear, there are times for righteous indignation, but that would still be meted out through those who bear the sword, as Paul says (Rom 13:4). I will address speaking with candor, frankness, or hardness in the next chapter, but the Holy Spirit, through Paul and James, tells you to put off words of sinful anger.

STRIFE/HOSTILITY/QUARRELING

Strife and hostility do not only manifest themselves in verbal forms, of course, but they do have a particular verbal essence embedded in their natures.[4] In strife, hostility, and quarreling, someone is offended or angered when their way of thinking isn't followed by another. And sinful humans prefer to have cronies lined up on their side, all rallying for the same cause. In a church setting, strife and hostility typically work through groupthink and mob mentality. One person gets upset, persuades others to join in, and then the whole group gets it in their corporate brain that "somebody has got to go!" It's executed with some measure of antagonism.[5] But long before the actual pushing out takes place, the hostility gets whipped up verbally. Strife, hostility, and quarrelling are all monumental wastes of kingdom time. The days are evil, and there is a Great Commission to pursue. We don't have time for lame pursuits like quarrelling—not to mention the disrepute it brings upon our Lord. Pastors are to be known by their love and forgiveness, not quarrelling. Put off hostility and strife.

FILTHY LANGUAGE

The debate over foul language continues to rage in American Christianity, and it goes something like this: "I am free in Christ. Therefore, cussing is acceptable behavior for me." Well, feast thine eyes on Ephesians 4:29, O free one! "No foul language should come from your mouth, but only what is good for building up someone in need." The question should never be, "what kind of foul-like talk can I get away with?" Instead it should be, "how might I steward and invest my whole life, including my words to build others up in the Lord?"

Your freedom was bought at a high price, and it means Christ is your master. Your master says, "obscene and foolish talking and crude joking are not suitable, but rather [pursue] giving thanks" (Eph 5:4). To talk crudely, obscenely, or unwholesomely is to speak indecently.[6] That is, if a culture accepts a word to be particularly profane, then we Christians ought to avoid that word. This isn't a hard concept, really; it's all about filling our mouths with good words instead of harmful ones. If you, or a few of your church members, are prone to indecent jesting—especially sexual—or unwholesome talk, you need to confess that to the Lord and ask for forgiveness and the strength to kill that sin pattern. Put off filthy language, pastor.

BLASPHEMY

Blasphemy can be tricky. It is manifested in quite a few ways, and sadly, we are not accustomed to speaking in terms of "blasphemy" these days. First, it is blasphemy to speak "emptily" of the Lord (Exod 20:7). That is to treat the Infinite and Almighty as though he were common—to drag him into the gutters of godless conversation, or to swear evil promises by invoking memory of his faithfulness. He is high, holy, and glorious—the complete opposite of ordinary—and to observe him in his grandeur would be to experience ruination! If we saw and comprehended his holiness, our moral offensiveness would be visibly highlighted, seen in high definition. Therefore, it seems that Satan is ever out and about, in each era and culture, to cause God's fallen and reconciled image bearers to speak of God as common, which is blasphemy.

Second, blasphemy can refer to denigrating something particularly holy or an image bearer. For instance, to slander about a particular local church or a fellow pastor would be to blaspheme. To gossip or speak maliciously of another person as though he or she were not immortal, image bearing, and God loved is to blaspheme. Fill your mouth with awe and praise of Jesus, brother. Put off blasphemy; it does not please the Lord.

LYING

In Titus 1:2 we are told that there is something God cannot do: God cannot lie. What would he gain by lying that he didn't already have? Our Triune God speaks and thinks and lives in absolute truth. And when you are hidden in Christ, you want and need for nothing. Lies accomplish only death. I wonder if you stretch the truth more than you recognize, pastor? Fill your life, mind, and mouth with the true truth of the Scriptures. We lie because we desire approval or worldly gain, so we speak untruths because we fear man instead of fearing God. But we should seek the approval of God over the approval of man. Await your "good and faithful servant" moment, brother. Seek the commendation of Christ. Put off worldly gain by putting off lying.

GRUMBLING/CRITICISM

In Numbers 12:1 Miriam and Aaron grumbled about Moses's leadership. They were blinded to all the kindnesses of the Lord wrought to them by means of their brother. In the end, we see it was an attempted power grab. It did not work out.

In Numbers 16 Korah did much the same. The result? Korah, his wife and kids, and many of his fellow mutineers died that day. Grumbling is the supreme attribute of the wilderness generation in Numbers and Deuteronomy. They grumble about the manna, the quail, Moses's leadership, and even entering the promised land (Num 13:31). Grumbling and godless criticism is totally anti-love and anti-thankfulness. In 2 Timothy 2:24 we are told that, "The Lord's servant must not quarrel, but must be gentle to everyone, able to teach, and patient, instructing his opponents with gentleness." You either already have or you will have opponents, pastor.

Do not fall to the sin pattern of grumbling, and especially don't grumble to other church members. Seek the Lord's face and ask that he grant you the gifts of thankfulness, patience, and gentleness. Put off grumbling; you will gain nothing of value from it.

FLATTERY

According to Paul, flattery leads to divisions in the church and creates obstacles to sanctification and healthy doctrine. Flatter-filled and flatter-prone people "do not serve our Lord Christ, but their own appetites, and by smooth talk and flattery they deceive the hearts of the naive" (Rom 16:18). Flattery is so dangerous because its sole purpose is to puff up, causing the carnival mirror effect wherein perception never quite equates to reality. It helps no one but only causes false worlds to be created in others. Instead, we need to praise the Lord, and speak with frankness, forthrightness, and love. Flattery is godless, graceless, and self-seeking; it is not for the good of another. There is more than enough to praise in another that does not include lying and its fraternal twin—flattery. Put off flattery, brother.

SARCASM

My wife has humorously dubbed sarcasm as "scarcasm." It is not a biblical term, but the way that sarcasm often manifests itself is certainly sinful. I don't mean to imply that there is never a time for a bit of skylarking. Elijah trolls the prophets of Baal with the best of them (1 Kgs 18), and Paul famously jests his desire that the false teachers in Galatia would emasculate themselves (Gal 5:12). It would seem, however, that the up-and-coming generations in the Western world are particularly prone to sarcasm. At its core, sarcasm involves taking a bit of truth and delivering it in a mocking, ironic, snarky, or condescending way, often with words or tone intended to harm or—at the very least—to merit a laugh at someone else's expense. And yet, it is a known, accepted, and expected gear of the heart that everyone has these days. I do not sense that it fits well with our call to mutual upbuilding, though (Eph 4:29). Sarcasm creates a kind of smoggy haze over our conversations—a haze that makes it hard to breathe the edifying air of kindness, affirmation, and encouragement. Put off sarcasm as a defining trait of who you are.

CONCLUSION

Well, that wasn't all that uplifting, was it? I know, I know. Here is the deal, though, pastor: we have to understand our sinful verbal impulses so that we can put them off and take on godly and loving talk. You are investing and stewarding your words for either life or death. You have to understand the enemy within and how he rears his ugly head so that you can know how to put to death the hurtful and death-bringing words from your lips. In the next chapter we will seek to understand and therefore deploy an array of healing words, so buckle up.

TIPS FOR YOUR TALK

TIP #1: DISCERN YOUR MOST PREVALENT AND TEMPTING FORM(S) OF VERBAL SIN.

Pastor, which two or three of these sins rendered above are your nemeses? What plan are you going to put in place so that you don't persist in them? The Lord intends for your mouth to be holy, which means you have work to do and sin to uproot. Have you invited anyone else in, maybe a fellow elder, to hold you accountable to putting these verbal sins under the knife of sanctification? Don't delay; today is the day of salvation! You can be clean if Jesus would but touch you with his cleansing power. Do some holy slaying of sin, brother. Christ has won the victory. Fight as though the battle is won, because it is. Beg and plead and prod your kind and benevolent Father to heal you.

TIP #2: PRAY YOUR CHURCH WOULD REPENT OF SLANDER, GOSSIP, AND MALICE.

What kind of talk typifies your church? I wonder what people around town think of your church? May it not be lost on you that your church's reputation—and how your church shapes Jesus's reputation in the minds of unbelievers—is well earned and largely displayed by how church members talk. Simple but true. Do people about town sense something distinct about the conversations they have with your members? Pray that the Lord would make your people salt and light. May the church you lead be distinct in its Christ-like talk.

TIP #3: WATCH OUT FOR SARCASM.

Sarcasm has a way of permeating everything. I challenge you to begin keeping tabs on how many of your conversations, and the conversations of your church members, are characterized by sarcasm. This we know: sarcasm creates an acidic atmosphere that chokes out kindness, affirmation, and encouragement. For the sake of Christ, his kingdom, and his church, it is probably best to eradicate it altogether. This is a tall order, but worthwhile.

THE PASTOR'S HEALING WORDS

Speaking Life

Therefore, if anyone is in Christ, he is a new creation; the old has passed away, and see, the new has come!"
—the apostle Paul

In the previous chapter we focused on the "fruit of the flesh," those kinds of words we know bring death. Having delineated and studied the words of the flesh, in this chapter my aim is to highlight the kind of words that bring life—even if at times received uncomfortably because they are difficult (e.g., admonishment). If you are going to invest and steward your words for life and not death, you must know how to shift into the gears of kindness, thanksgiving, affirmation, and godly correction and away from sinful speech.

As we've already established, and at the risk of beating a dead horse, in most of Paul's letters a recognizable pattern emerges wherein he distinguishes the works and words of the flesh from the works and the words of the Spirit. He places two different lives in stark contrast, and this is meant for our instruction in godliness. Furthermore, the Holy Spirit's intent in structuring many of Paul's letters this way is to make it easy to discern who is and who isn't Christian by showing what a Christian does and doesn't say. In Colossians 3:8 Paul writes, "But now, put away all the following: anger, wrath, malice, slander, and filthy language from your mouth." So then, those are the types and categories of words and communication the Christian should "put away." The categories of words we are to "put on" are words of "kindness, humility, gentleness, and patience" (Col 3:12). Furthermore, we are to, "Let the word of Christ dwell richly among [us], in all wisdom teaching and admonishing one another through psalms, hymns, and spiritual songs, singing to God with gratitude in [our] hearts" (3:16).

In Ephesians 4:31 Paul explains it like this: "Let all bitterness and wrath and anger and clamour and slander be put away from you along with all malice," and in 5:4, "Let there be no filthiness nor foolish talk nor crude joking, which are out of place, but instead let there be thanksgiving." Notice the phrase "put away" and the word "instead." Paul intends for the Christian to forsake some things, the former manner of living, and to exchange those things for a new way of life. Let us now look to the categories and forms of communication we are to put on. My aim is not to exhaust this category of life-giving speech, but I do aim to be sufficiently comprehensive so you can distinguish and then choose between fleshly, death-bringing talk and Spirit-filled, life-giving talk.

KINDNESS

To speak kindly means to deliver a beneficial word of some kind without caveat or expecting anything in return.[7] There is a dearth of kindness in our world, wouldn't you agree? The world can be a cold and comfortless place, but if our churches and homes are places of kindness, then they are pillows for the soul. They will be spaces of restitution and hope—a foretaste of a future-coming, wholesome, sinless, deathless, resurrected new earth and heavens where kindness will be the constant environs. When we speak kindly to one another, we enact and usher in that next realm.

Pastor, have you ever had someone say something truly kind to you? Try to remember it now. Was it not to you as pure, cool water on the parched throat of your soul? To receive a kind word in this life is utterly otherworldly and countercultural. Screeds and harangues, lectures and diatribes are the norm in our litigious, hate-filled age. Not so in the church of our Lord Jesus Christ. Kindness is king because our King has been supremely kind to us. Choose to speak kindly, pastor. The world and your congregation desperately need it. They are exposed all day long to the brutal elements of the vicious atmosphere that permeates a lost culture. Therefore, bring them kindness with no recourse or expectation. Put on words of kindness.

THANKSGIVING

The Christian possesses nearly an infinite number of things for which he or she can be thankful. We can thank God for putting death to death. We can thank God for his saving us when we were in defiance of him and resolute in our sins. We can thank God for the Scriptures that light our path. We can thank him for so many good Bible translations that help us to understand God as he is revealed in his Word. We can thank God for whatever measure of health we have, as he continues to give us breath for today. We can thank God for not running out on us (Jude 24–25). We can thank God for our spouse, children, grandchildren, parents, and siblings. I am thankful God gave me parents who took me to church and diligently disciplined me.

I don't deserve any of these things. You don't deserve even one, single kindness that has come to you. Fill your mouth with thankfulness, and you'll crowd out grumbling, slander, gossip, and anger. I am often surprised by how quickly I can downshift into negativity and groaning. Brother, it should not be so. When we live in Christ's light and life, we are awakened to all we have to be thankful for. Be the kind of pastor that unconverted image bearers, your family, and church members long to be around. You know when that will happen? When they find you to be utterly otherworldly in your thankfulness, an alien meant for another world. Be thankful.

AFFIRMATION

If thankfulness is a state or posture of the heart, then affirmation is a declarative statement about the current state of a person. To affirm someone is to express that you see God at work in their life or to confirm that you see God using them in this or that way. Affirmation does not expect anything in response; it simply declares a truth about another human being. Like an engine receiving a nitrous oxide boost, affirmation can only do the Christian good.

Abigail spoke affirmation to David in order to calm him in his rage against her fool husband, Nabal. She says,

> My lord should pay no attention to this worthless fool Nabal, for he lives up to his name: His name means "stupid," and stupidity is all he knows. I, your servant, didn't see my lord's young men whom you sent.... Please forgive your servant's offense, for the Lord is certain to make a lasting dynasty for my lord because he fights the Lord's battles. Throughout your life, may evil not be found in you.... My lord's life is tucked safely in the place where the Lord your God protects the living, but he is flinging away your enemies' lives like stones from a sling. When the Lord does for my lord all the good he promised you and appoints you ruler over Israel, there will not be remorse or a troubled conscience for my lord because of needless bloodshed or my lord's revenge. And when the Lord does good things for my lord, may you remember me your servant.
> (1 Sam 25:25–31)

NO NEUTRAL WORDS

Abigail uses her words to affirm David. She knows something that David seems to have lost at this moment: namely that, as one hidden in the Lord, he is more honorable than his present course of action would indicate. She does this by affirming all the promises of God in David's life. Her affirmation is powerful, future looking, compelling, and declarative. A steady diet of affirmation is what a person who is depressed or anxious needs more than anything else. Many times we shove encouragement down their throat, which has its place, but what a melancholy or anxious person needs to know is that, even in the pit, God is at work. Affirm one another.

ENCOURAGEMENT

If thankfulness is a heart posture, and affirmation is declarative in nature, then encouragement is more of a cheerleader. Encouragement intends to draw us mentally away from the present difficulty or trial by casting our minds to the saving activity of God in our past, that we would be strengthened for the future. It is a cheerleader, then. It roots us onward. It builds our confidence in God's saving work. It equips us with right-sized and rightly oriented courage. It is a shot of electrolytes to the soul.

When Paul writes to Timothy, "For I am already being poured out as a drink offering, and the time of my departure is close. . . . Demas has deserted me. . . . Alexander the coppersmith did great harm to me. . . . [A]t my defense no one stood by me, but everyone deserted me" (2 Tim 4:6–16), he was in great need of encouragement. If Timothy had been

THE PASTOR'S HEALING WORDS

physically present with Paul, he surely would have beat Paul to the punch and reminded him, "[you] have fought the good fight. [You] have finished the race. [You] have kept the faith. There is reserved for [you] the crown of righteousness." Paul needed encouragement running through the veins of his soul. Likewise, your church members, wife, children, and neighbors need to be encouraged by the hope found in the fact that Jesus has overcome the world, the flesh, and the Devil. Encouragement flags us on in the race. It shouts and points to the finish line, saying, "Keep going . . . keep evangelizing . . . keep praying . . . keep believing . . . keep confessing . . . keep fighting, you precious Saint of God." Put on encouragement.

COMMENDATION

Commendation is the godly version of flattery. Really, it is the opposite of flattery, because commendation is grounded in truth, not puff, and it seeks to do good to all who hear it. Paul, leveraging his apostolic authority, commends Epaphras to the local church in Colossae in Colossians 1:7. While all commendation should be encouraging, not all encouragement is commendation. Commendation speaks truth both to the one needing the encouragement and to all those who hear the commendation.

Most of us walk around in the dark as to whether God is really using us, and we also walk around somewhat suffocated by a lack of love felt through encouragement and affirmation. Commendation is a powerful tool in the hands of a pastor.

When you see someone growing in godliness or doing that which is godly, commend them publicly. They will feel loved. Your church will see an example of godly sanctification, and you will be a powerful means of God's love to all of them.

SPEAKING PEACE

Making peace between church members assumes mediation through the vehicle of words. In Romans 12:18 we are told, "If possible, as far as it depends on you, live at peace with everyone." In order for you to fulfill this wise and holy counsel, you must be gracious, measured, and *for others* in your speech. To have peace in your church takes an extraordinary level of attentiveness and care. You and your fellow elders will need to constantly model this. You will have to show your members that you can disagree in an agreeable and peaceful way. Maintaining peace in your church, home, and relationships does not mean no one ever disagrees, but it does mean that all involved uphold a hearty commitment to biblical paradigms of authority and that everyone is ever ready to make reconciliation when there is a fissure.

SINGING

In Colossians 3:16 and elsewhere, Paul alerts us to the importance of filling our mouths with singing instead of sinning: Paul says, "Let the word of Christ dwell richly among you . . . admonishing one another through psalms, hymns, and spiritual songs, singing to God with gratitude in your hearts." First, notice that this is a congregational command. Your Lord expects—even demands!—that you sing as a church. It is pivotal for you and your congregation's fight against sin that you sing. This is why singing doctrinally rich lyrics is so paramount. Singing is warfare. Second, notice that this command does not have to be relegated to Sunday morning. Sing at home in family worship. Sing in the morning. Sing in the evening. As a family, I would suggest singing small portions of "Holy, Holy, Holy" and "This is the Day that the Lord has Made" to consecrate each day to the Lord and to calibrate your home to life lived in Christ.

CONFESSING

God tells us through the pen of James that local church members are to "confess [our] sins to one another." James is not the only place we are told to do this. As pastor, be the exemplar in your church in being the first to confess sin as articulated in Colossians 3:5–10 and Galatians 5:19–21. Show your family and your church that to be a Christian pastor is not to be perfect, but to be repentant.

ADMONISHMENT

All the previous modes of communication covered in this chapter have been "positive," if you will, in nature. The next three typically sting a bit, but they are absolutely essential in a fallen world. One day, when we rise in our Lord, there will be no need for admonishment, correction, or rebuke. But in this realm they are essential. If you avoid them altogether, you will commit yourself to a very unfaithful ministry, if you do not disqualify yourself in the process. That said, the end goal of these modes of speaking life, like church discipline (Matt 18:15–20), is ultimately restoration.

The meaning of admonishment is broad, but at its simplest it means to teach, instruct, or correct by means of words.[8] When applied to a child in the home, it can take on disciplinary elements. We ought to deploy admonishment when we see a church member persisting in sin or when someone we care about is pursuing foolishness or laziness. It should be calculated and measured, never harsh or off key. Admonishment aims to propel the other toward godliness and never condemnation. To sit someone down and admonish them is holy and serious. Do not take it lightly. Follow up with affirmation, encouragement, thankfulness, and care, lest you push them toward bitterness or undue discouragement.

CORRECTION/GODLY CONFRONTATION

To correct someone assumes something is out of sorts. Something is, in fact, incorrect. Therefore, if you were to biblically correct someone, it would inherently mean you discovered an error or erring way, *not* that you went on an expedition in search of faults.[9] Correction, like admonishment, is never waltzed into lightly. It is not something to revel in or enjoy. It is necessary, hard, and yet loving if done well.

Correction ("confronted" or "opposed")[10] is what Paul uses in Galatians 2:11-13 when he discovers that Peter is leading the Jews, and even Barnabas, into gospel-less racism ("hypocrisy"). The key to note in Galatians is that Paul employs his strong opposition by "speak[ing] the truth in love." The whole episode is covered in the hope of redemption and always with a tenor of grace. Paul doesn't trash Peter but instead speaks directly and frankly in order to bring about gospel purity and restoration.

Brother-pastor, is there a longstanding conversation you've been avoiding that calls for correction? Do you fear the Lord enough to offend someone for their own good? Be ready to correct lovingly when needed.

REBUKE

We are in great need of straightforward, frank, candid talk today. We are a people—both inside and outside the church—who are filled with pride and puff. I suspect we struggle in this way because the majority of us have never experienced much corporate or societal suffering. That is a formula for ego inflation and misguided self-perception. We desperately need men and women in the ministry who will speak straightforwardly and frankly about the bitter harvest that sin brings, both in this life and the next.

In 1 Timothy 1:19-20 Paul publicly rebukes by name Hymenaeus and Alexander. He straightforwardly and forcefully writes that he has delivered them over "to Satan, so that they may be taught not to blaspheme." You gotta love

Paul! The man rarely falls to the sin of being contentious, but he also knew when it was time to have a scrap. But even here with these contemptuous false teachers, we see Paul's compassion and empathy. He says much the same in the context of church discipline in 1 Corinthians 5:5 when he says, "hand that one over," the brazenly sexually immoral one, "to Satan for the destruction of his flesh, *so that his spirit may be saved in the day of the Lord.*" Paul was holding out for restoration.

It would seem a safe bet, even here in 1 Timothy, that Paul is punching hard at Hymenaeus and Alexander with tears in his eyes. He hopes the rebuke will wake them up, jolt them into seeing the degenerate state of their souls. But this is no glancing blow; Paul comes at them head on. These false teachers used their words to hurt the local church in Ephesus. Rebuke, especially public rebuke, is reserved for tough times like this when public sin calls for public correction. Yet it is a broad sword, and usually comes accompanied by significant collateral damage. While the damage is never ideal, we rebuke because it's right and good and, Lord willing, restorative for those caught in the crossfire.

Rebuke, however, is not reserved for false teachers only. In Titus 2 Paul tells Titus to "encourage and rebuke with all authority. Let no one disregard you" (2:15). Right after this, Paul pours steel into Titus's spine by saying, "avoid foolish debates, genealogies, quarrels, and disputes about the law, because they are unprofitable and worthless. *Reject* a divisive person after a first and second warning. For you know that such a person has gone astray and is sinning; he is self-condemned." That term "reject" most typically means to warn or correct.[11] In this case, Paul applies it to divisive church members in the local church in Crete.

Pastor, much is on the line when we consider the weightiness of our charge. We are tasked with being watchmen over the fidelity of the gospel, pure doctrine, the execution of justice in love, and the great commission of our Lord. At times you will have to rebuke people in love. Never go lightly into these matters, but do not shy away from them either.

CONCLUSION

As you can see, you have an overabundance of Christ-exalting communicative tools in your belt. There is no reason to invest your words in the bank account of death—nor any reason to steward your words poorly—thereby producing spiritual casualty in those around you.

TIPS FOR YOUR TALK

TIP #1: READ SAM CRABTREE'S *PRACTICING AFFIRMATION: GOD-CENTERED PRAISE OF THOSE WHO ARE NOT GOD.*

Without question, *Practicing Affirmation* is the most useful book I've encountered on the subject of choosing our words to heal instead of hurt. Do yourself and those around you a favor and pick this book up as soon as possible. Read it. Mark it up. Apply it. Read it again. Seek to apply it to specific people in your life.

TIP #2: PRACTICE THESE SIX DIFFERENT WAYS TO SPEAK LIFE TODAY

First, thank God for five eternal things he has given you in Christ. Second, email a friend and bless them with an encouraging word. Third, call a church member and affirm them in their labors for the Lord. Fourth, text one or both of your parents (or maybe a sibling) and speak a kind word to them. Fifth, set up that meeting you've been avoiding. Maybe it's time to talk it out in hopes of finding peace. Sixth, make these prayers, emails, calls, texts, and meetings the norm, pastor.

PART FOUR

THE PASTOR'S WORDS IN THE TWENTY FIRST CENTURY

THE PASTOR'S SOCIAL MEDIA WORDS

The digital age is part gift and part curse. Facebook, Twitter, Instagram, Snapchat, and Pinterest, plus any of the other social media platforms that exist by the time this book reaches your hands, *ad infinitum*, all enable your words to go further and faster than ever before. The digital age is a gift if our words are good and constructive, but it is a curse if we use social media channels for destruction. Either way, the truth stands: The digital age, and social media more specifically, is a monumental stewardship.

SOCIAL MEDIA PLATFORMS ARE NOT NEUTRAL MEDIUMS

I sometimes wonder if, in thirty or forty years, we'll look back on smartphones and social media like we look back on the proliferation of cigarette use back in the 50s and 60s ("Oh, I don't know, honey. Those cigarettes seem pretty harmless to me. He's thirteen. Let him light one up with his friends. Don't embarrass him."). The cavalier attitude toward smoking then would be viewed as reckless and callous now, and I anticipate we may feel similarly toward our reliance on our smart devices in a few decades. My suspicion is that we weren't meant to have a soul so intertwined with a digital device. But what do I know? I'm no neuroscientist.

Here is what I do know. Our words function much like extensions of our person, of our leadership. We release them and then they are just out there, floating in eternal time and space like little tentacles that branch off of our ministries. In Matthew 12:33–37 we saw that none of our words, not even one, fails to reach the divine ears of God. Nor do any of our words escape his impeccable memory. Because of the digital age and the phenomenon of social media, your words now have a disproportionate influence beyond your physical space. Further, your digital footprint, your word ministry online, piles up on itself in a way that would have astounded your forebears. The internet, and social media more particularly, is unwieldy, unyielding, restless, relentless, instant, and permanent. Once you have posted something, it's nearly impossible to pull it back down.

This pixelated cyber soil that we minister and grow in has become fertile for all manner of wordish sins. It is not a neutral platform. You already know that, though, don't you? Even when something doesn't technically go viral, it can still *feel* viral even if its localized to our own circles. The people you pastor are often hurt on social media and rarely built up. But you, pastor, must be vigilant and keep your social media words Godward. We can't rewind time, though. There is no virtue in crying over the digital spilled milk of our age, and there is no hope of bringing back a bygone era before these platforms existed (Eccl 7:10). And frankly, social media isn't the main problem anyway. Your heart is!

Social media platforms just happen to be the latest and greatest stage upon which we let our depraved tongues do their dancing. I propose, as it pertains to social media, that many of us should just post a lot less. Just cut your words (posts and comments) down by 50-75 percent. Proverbs 10:19 provides us with a good rule of thumb: "When there are many words, sin is unavoidable, but the one who controls his lips is prudent." We shouldn't let the accessibility of a platform delude us into thinking we know something about this or that. We are not experts or authorities on most things, so the safe, conservative bet is to keep our mouths more closed than open, digitally speaking. At the very least, we ought to exercise a thimble full of patience and wait until we have gathered all the necessary information available on whatever recent scuttlebutt we wish to pontificate on.

ON KEYBOARD COWBOYS AND TWITTER TROLLS

If ol' King Solomon were still penning Proverbs today, he might have included one or two proverbs like this (let the reader understand):

Don't answer a troll according to his trolling or you too will become trollful.

Answer a keyboard cowboy according to his foolishness, or he'll become wise in his own eyes.

I am convinced that social media foolishness fits firmly into the category of Proverbs 26:4, wherein we are told not to answer a fool according to his folly, lest in the end we are found to wallow around in the same ditch of foolishness with him. Furthermore, I am increasingly convinced that a lot of the foolishness on social media is just that—foolishness. And you know who commit foolishness? Fools.

If a professing believer constantly vents their anger on social media but doesn't have hard, face-to-face conversations with people they disagree with, then they are malnourished Christians. They ought to be pitied, prayed for, and mentored, but not engaged. Engaging trolls—also known as jerks!—on their playing field gives them something of an endorphin kick. Don't train them to love it more than they already do. If anything, seek to take things offline and have a personal conversation with them where you bring them to a level of understanding through love and candor. Pastor, whatever you do, do not become the fool online. You will hurt your ministry with actual people by being rude and vitriolic online.

ON TWITTER PASTORS AND THE LIKE

Another social media phenomenon I have noticed is that of the "Twitter pastor." The Twitter pastor is a pastor somewhere, and you've likely never met him. But when you sit down to check your socials, the whole thing is filled up with posts and responses from this "social media Pastor." This is really a pitiable thing. His church members are hard at work, by God's grace, doing the work of the ministry, while he sits posted up in cyber space cackling and giggling with his buddies. He thinks to himself, "All of Pinterest is my parish." He's the guy who digitally bounds over state and church covenant boundaries to slap this or that church member or fellow pastor on the hand for holding this or that position or for not speaking up about this or that subject. Pastor, do not become this guy. If you already are—or you suspect you might be—take a break from social media for a while, reduce your platforms down to only one, or delete your accounts altogether. Ninety-nine percent of ministry is done face-to-face or in conversation on the phone. You do not NEED social media.

CONCLUSION

Social media has a way of making us feel ten feet tall and bullet proof. It is prone to puff us up, it isn't neutral, and some of us just can't be trusted with it. If you are one of these people (half the time I am!), that is not a bad thing. It is just reality. Your sanctification is not worth sacrificing on the altar of a smartphone app. Social media is not a right but a privilege of the particularly sanctified. If you are prone to being the Twitter pastor or keyboard cowboy, you will stand in judgment for that. Your social media words are not precluded from what Jesus says in Matthew 12:34–37: "For the mouth speaks from the overflow of the heart. . . . I tell you that on the day of judgment people will have to account for every careless word they speak. For by your words you will be acquitted, and by your words you will be condemned."

TIPS FOR YOUR TALK

TIP #1: SPEND MORE TIME IN CONVERSATION WITH PEOPLE IN YOUR CHURCH AND NEIGHBORHOOD THAN ON SOCIAL MEDIA.

Most of ministry is done face-to-face or over the phone, and it ought to be so. A good rule of thumb is that the closer you are physically, the more meaningful the pastoral impact. A phone call is more impactful than a text and a text more impactful than a tweet. In-person conversation trumps them all.

TIP #2: CONSIDER REDUCING YOUR SOCIAL MEDIA USAGE TO JUST ONE PLATFORM.

This is how I have sought to manage the madness personally. I am on Twitter, but I am not on Facebook, Instagram, etc. In addition to saving you time in checking all of the platforms for updates, you'll be limited in the number of ways you can use your words for death. Come on over here to my lane; the jaunt is just fine.

TIP #3: DON'T ENGAGE TROLLS. EVER. EVEN IF THEY COME AFTER YOU.

This really doesn't need any qualifying, but for the sake of clarity, answering jerks, trolls, and fools online only brings the nobility of the pastorate down. If a heretic, false teacher, or juvenile fool is ranting or pontificating, don't join in! You will be healthier and better for it. If you know them personally and can move them in some way, then do so *offline*. Finally, encourage your church members to stay away from those patterns of social media communication.

TIP #4: TURN OFF YOUR NOTIFICATIONS.

Pastor, you will not be able to stay synced up healthily with multiple social media channels at all times. I suggest you remove all notifications so you can control when you receive information instead of being controlled and constantly pinged by your social media portals. Turning off my notifications has drastically changed the way I take in Twitter.

TIP #5: MAKE SOCIAL MEDIA A REGULAR PART OF YOUR SERMON APPLICATION.

Yes, I am an old curmudgeon, but I am not a dope. Social media mediums are here to stay, and they are a major part of your church members lives. Therefore, you ought to help shape the way they think about that avenue of their life while in the pulpit by means of the sacred Scriptures. If you expect them to be sanctified on social media, help them know how.

9

THE PASTOR'S FUNNY WORDS

We live in a particularly comedic era—the era of YouTube goofs, GIFs, dad jokes, and stand-up comedy. Technological shifts have afforded us societal consumption of humor in ways that would have staggered former generations. In many ways, our lives are completely different from former generations.

The digital age has created an appetite for constant jesting such that you, your church members, and most everyone you meet has a pent-up desire to laugh at almost anything. My suspicion is that this is the case because we are so hollowed out and heartbroken in our sin that we medicate with massive quantities of humor. Don't get me wrong; most of the time I love landing a good joke—more than the next guy, actually. And if you were to poll those closest to me, they would likely say that Sam constantly flies between the poles of being embarrassingly silly (verging on corny?) and supremely serious. I am no stranger to that kind of laughter that breaks into salty tears and makes your stomach hurt. However, many parts of life—funerals, hell, joblessness, miscarriages, barrenness, divorce, drug addiction, disease, defiant children, or cancer, to instance a few—are not funny at all. With our words, pastor, we must never become so addicted to humor that we squeeze out the biblically allotted space for pain, lament, and biblical grief.

ON HUMOR IN THE PULPIT

You must know that the members of your church come expecting jokes from the pulpit on Sundays. But here is the issue: the most important and eternal things in our lives are not humorous. Humor is of third-rate—at most second-rate—importance within the kingdom of God. At Liberty Baptist Church where I pastor, my fellow brother-pastors and I are no strangers to a bit of humor in the pulpit. But it must be said, we need far more sobriety in the pulpit than humor. Most of the Bible is not humorous. It is filled with the constant clashing of the titanic realities of heaven and hell. This is what hangs in the balance every time you mount the pulpit. Our people need us to take seriously their sin and their salvation.

ON HUMOR AND SOCIAL MEDIA

If I am arguing that the pulpit ought to be primarily reserved for more serious matters of God, and if you still find yourself to be of the humorous type, then social media is where you can really shine, brother. There is no end of cat videos and funny flops to repost. With that said, the two key questions to ask yourself are: (1) Is what I am about to post potentially spiteful or hurtful to a fellow image bearer, group, or entity? In other words, who am I hurting with this comment or video? It may be very funny, but that does not mean it is holy. (2) Is what I am about to post for the mutual upbuilding of the church? Does this content equip and encourage others toward maturity in Christ?

Now, pastor, if you are a keyboard cowboy or Twitter pastor, then you most likely need to take a three-month sabbatical from social media, or maybe delete your accounts altogether. Here's why I can forthrightly say that: divisiveness and attacking other blood-bought Christians before a watching world is never funny; it's deplorable. Christ was pinned to a cross and died for that divisive post. How dare you treat it as trivial. You need to turn from your sin patterns, sir. Maybe this is one of those moments where you cut your keyboard off at the cord or gauge out your social media eye.

I try to be humorous, encouraging, informative, and benign on social media. For the humor part, I try to make sure someone somewhere is not wincing because of my humor. Beyond that, keep your channels benevolent and Christward.

ON HUMOR IN CONVERSATION

Cracking funnies, as I hope we've established, is great. A holy people ought to be a people who can laugh and not take their reputation too seriously. In conversation, then, consider which generation, culture, and background the person(s) you are conversing with belong to. Try to understand conversational decorum and how things will be received. This *is* love. You are dying to self and your desires. And who rises in the ashes of that small death to self? The person you are conversing with. Even if the only person who ever notices is God, do it anyway. Love people and slay yourself by putting their communicative needs and wants in front of your own.

CONCLUSION

The cross and resurrection of Jesus Christ is no laughing matter. But, every holy and side-splitting moment of laughter you get in this life is a blood-bought gift. What a kindness humor is, but don't let it crowd out lament and sorrow. There is room for both.

TIPS FOR YOUR TALK

TIP #1: MAKE SURE PEOPLE DON'T WALK AWAY FROM YOUR SERMONS THINKING THAT YOU'RE FUNNY BUT FAILING TO REMEMBER THE TEXT OR THE CROSS.

I am no killjoy, but if your church members walk away from your preaching first glorying in the witty and humorous things you said and only secondly glorying in the truths of the text and the cross of Christ, brother, you have failed in your calling. Curtail your humor and lift high your saving God. May he soar over your sermons and may your earth-bound humor play second, fifth, or even seventh fiddle.

TIP #2: IN CONVERSATION, BE JOVIAL AND YET RESPECTFUL AND THOUGHTFUL.

In conversation, you have an incredible opportunity to die to yourself so that others might live. Conversation is one way in which you can serve others. Adhere to their mode of conversation. Ask them questions. Seek to understand them, hope the best, and gently push them toward Christ at all times.

TIP #3: KNOW THAT YOUR PEOPLE HAVE A PENT-UP DESIRE TO LAUGH AT ALL TIMES.

This is likely because we hide pain and sorrow behind a mask of laughter. Why else have so many high-profile comedians overdosed and taken their lives? The soul cannot survive in an ecosystem that thrives on cynicism and sarcasm or in one only intent on finding that next hit of laughter. Make room for the serious. Your people need it.

EPILOGUE

Sometimes, before I enter into the pulpit to preach, I am reminded of Hebrews 10:31: "It is a terrifying thing to fall into the hands of the living God." And I'm reminded of 12:29: "Our God is a consuming fire." And I pray, "O God! You would be absolutely just and righteous to kill me in this pulpit." I am that sinful. My mouth, just like Isaiah's, is morally repulsive and unclean. If you don't sense or believe that too, pastor, then you need to start over at the beginning of this book. There is no more dangerous place in all the world than to be elevated five feet up on a platform—suspended between heaven and earth, between a holy God and his people—speaking on behalf of this holy God. To preach with such unclean lips is an audacious and frightening charge.

I have realized through the writing of this book that a close second to being suspended between God and man in the pulpit is the call to minister to God's people on God's behalf. We are, as 1 Timothy 3:1-7 indicates, called of God himself to shepherd his flock. What is more, in Revelation 2:1, Jesus "walks among" his churches. That is both frightening and heartening. What this means is that every word we expend in this world as ambassadors of Christ counts—it is known.

We are investing in the bank accounts of those around us for either death or life, constantly making deposits. No word is neutral. Jesus can and will save you from your sinful speech patterns. You only have to ask him and then humbly give yourself over to the arduous, lifelong, painful process of sanctification in this area. The more sanctified your mouth, the more edifying a pastor you will be. Jesus is good; he *will* save you.

ENDNOTES

[1] John MacArthur, *The Vanishing Conscience: Drawing the Line in a No-Fault, Guilt-Free World* (Dallas: Word, 1994), 39.

[2] J. P. Louw, and E. A. Nida, *Greek-English lexicon of the New Testament: Based on Semantic Domains*, 2nd ed., 2 vols. (New York: United Bible Societies, 1996), 1:433.

[3] Louw and Nida, *Greek-English Lexicon*, 1:434.

[4] Louw and Nida, *Greek-English Lexicon*, 1:494.

[5] Louw and Nida, *Greek-English Lexicon*, 1:437.

[6] Louw and Nida, *Greek-English Lexicon*, 1:392.

[7] Louw and Nida, *Greek-English Lexicon*, 1:749.

[8] Louw and Nida, *Greek-English Lexicon*, 1:414.

[9] Louw and Nida, *Greek-English Lexicon*, 1:673.

[10] Louw and Nida, *Greek-English Lexicon*, 1:491.

[11] Louw and Nida, *Greek-English Lexicon*, 1:414.

Made in the USA
Monee, IL
07 March 2023